£7·50

3

D1075246

THE DECLINE OF DEMOCRACY

RALPH BUULTJENS, a distinguished political scientist and leading scholar of Asian philosophy, was born in Sri Lanka (Ceylon) and now lives in the United States. He has had affiliations with several research and educational institutions around the world and his writings and media work have received wide recognition. Professor Buultjens teaches international politics and philosophy at the New School for Social Research and at Maryknoll Graduate School of Theology and is visiting professor at Pace University (Graduate School) and the International Study and Research Institute in New York. His publications include *Traditional Faiths and Asian Development, Buddhist Doctrine and Dogma—The Challenge of Change*, and, most recently, *Rebuilding the Temple: Tradition and Change in Modern Asia*. Dr. Buultjens is currently Chairman of the International Development Forum, a worldwide group of eminent social scientists and scholars, and was formerly president of the Society for International Development (New York). Chairman of both the New York Buddhist Council and the Council of Asian Affairs, he is also Honorary Minister of the New York Buddhist Church and serves as special adviser and consultant to several international organizations.

THE DECLINE
OF DEMOCRACY

*Essays on an
Endangered Political Species*

RALPH BUULTJENS

Library of Congress Cataloging in Publication Data

Buultjens, Ralph.
  The decline of democracy.

    1. Democracy—Addresses, essays, lectures.
I. Title.
JC423.B93   321.8   77-13276
ISBN 0-88344-080-6
ISBN 0-88344-081-4 pbk.

FOR PET

So much, so little

CONTENTS

APPENDIX 2: SELECTED QUOTATIONS ON DEMOCRACY

Preface

From time to time, academicians need to abandon the rigors of their specialties and reflect on the broader environment of their vocations and disciplines. This book is the result of a period of such reflection. In many ways, it has been a painful experience, a reassessment of assumptions that have formed the bedrock of my thinking on political systems and the social order of our era.

Intellectual conviction and personal circumstance have long led me to believe that democracy is the most enlightened, effective, and forward-looking philosophy of government. It has flaws and problems, but I was confident that the appeal of its rationality and justice would eventually prevail. Preparation of these essays has made me question this faith. The values of democracy have little relevance for most of the world's peoples today. Of its effectiveness, there is now much doubt, and its future is more uncertain than at any time in recent history. I do not make these observations in a mood of pessimism, but I know that objective analysis requires an appreciation and a presentation of reality. And I have a troubling sensation that we are living in a period that future scholars may come to regard as the twilight years of democracy. The prospect that political habits that have been so widely accepted will recede into history is not an ebullient one.

It is my view that part of the reason for this decline is a weakness in education. There is little continuing or serious concern for educating students or citizens about the condition and the responsibilities of democracy. Occasional controversy provokes intense discussion in the news media, but this dissipates as more current topics capture its attention. Many universities and colleges list courses on Marxism, socialism, military politics, and the like, but very few offer any on democracy. A library search indicates a similar disproportion between publications on other ideologies and those on democracy. This inadequacy of instruction must result in an inadequacy of understanding and practice; it contrasts strongly with the high priority nondemocratic nations give to teaching the philosophic underpinnings of their regimes.

These essays, and the documents and selected quotations that are appended, are not a comprehensive attempt to meet this need, nor are they academic surveys or historical studies. What I have tried to address are some of the central themes and urgencies of modern democracy. This is a personal retrospect: one man's lonely attempt to retrace his intellectual path. It is an effort, I dare to hope, that will provide insights that others may find useful.

Along this journey there have been several way stations. The International Study and Research Institute, in New York, invited me to deliver a series of lectures on democracy and so helped formulate my ideas. Students at the New School for Social Research, Maryknoll Seminary, Pace University, and Marymount Manhattan College were a patient testing-ground for some of these concepts. My colleagues at the International Development Forum have informed and enriched my thinking. While they and others did contribute much, this work is essentially the product of many hours of introspection. Responsibility for its weaknesses and its strengths is ultimately mine alone.

RALPH BUULTJENS

New York City
November 1977

Introduction

Democracy has many meanings and takes many shapes; it has existed under many conditions and is practiced in many ideologically diverse nations. These essays concern that type of democracy which has become principally identified with modern industrial societies—a political system first established in the United States in the late eighteenth century and also increasingly incorporated into the British form of government around that time. Although the forms and mechanisms it employs are its most obvious characteristics, it has, as we shall see, a distinctive philosophical content. Additionally, in certain uses it has become identified with certain economic systems or outlooks. Indeed, political scientists and others now often refer to this system as "capitalist democracy" or "western-oriented democracy." These statements are often polemic and require some refinement. The need for definition also comes from a problem of communication; in focusing on "democracy," it became evident to me that this term evokes several levels of response and has several shadings of meaning. As I began to construct a starting point, I found that my framework of definition contained two elements—a generally accepted, disciplinary description, and more subjective guidelines drawn from personal perspectives and study. Thinking and writing about the problems of government merged these perceptions into the following concepts, which I have used as my general criteria of democracy throughout this volume.

Democracy, as it has evolved through theory and practice, now signifies a political environment in which several general conditions exist. I believe that four of

1

these are of particular importance. The first is an observance of the rights of political choice through regular, open, and contested elections. Although special circumstances may occasionally necessitate deferrals of elections, the centerpiece of democracy involves a free and relatively frequent selection process in which opposing groups have broadly similar access to the voting public. A fundamental part of this condition is the absence of special pressures or coercive influences in favor of some groups or persons at the expense of others.

A second and related circumstance involves the existence and participation of genuine opposition forces. This situation may also require modification when elements of the polity express their dissent in criminal or destructive ways. However, in a democratic environment, restrictions placed on opposition should be determined by judicial or other objective processes, supported by public evidence, and not by the whims of those who govern.

My third criteria relates to the expression of dissent. The reflection of dissent in the instruments of public communication and through public assembly is a classic test of the working condition of democracy. These instruments—the press, radio, television, and other media—must be nonpartisan politically or must be available to a variety of opposing views. Imposed controls vitiate democratic practices.

A fourth and more obvious condition is the scope of the democratic political system. Democracy confined to a narrow segment of the national population can scarcely qualify for consideration as a form whose very name suggests the inclusion of as many citizens as possible. There are many inconsistencies in this or in most other visions of democracy at work. Among those which flaw my definition are the inherent contradictions present in constitutional monarchies; the paradox of essentially one-party governments allowing relatively free and regular elections; military support being used to keep democratic regimes in power against strong and undemocratic opposition; systems in which a genuine democracy prevails for only one portion of the population. Recent political events and situations in countries as different as Australia, Mexico, India, Turkey, South Africa, and Israel illustrate that these are not abstract problems or theoretical paradoxes. Although these and other imprecisions inhibit a clearer initial demarcation of the term "democracy," I have tried to convey a more defined perception through discussions of the components of democracy in these essays.

Using this preliminary definition of democracy, one finds that in today's world, out of nearly 160 countries, there are approximately twenty-three which observe these customs, whose governments, at least apparently, can be changed through the electoral process. This is a smaller number than at any recent time, and news reports suggest that even it is shrinking; in both size and integrity, democracy is surely an endangered political species. India, after the national elections of March 1977, is technically the largest of these nations. However, the fragility of democracy in India was illustrated by the ease with which it was suspended in mid-1975 and its durability must be regarded as tentative. The United States, with its population of approximately 215 million (almost one-third that of India), has had the longest continuous history of democratic government and of stable democratic political institutions. Next in size comes Japan with approximately one-half of this population. A cluster of Western European states, each with about one-half the population of Japan, follow: Britain, France, West Germany, Italy. Thereafter are a group of small nations, mostly also located in Europe. Canada, and perhaps Mexico, must be counted in North America. Australia, New Zealand, and a few others are all that remain.

In a very real sense, then, the United States is the last major bastion of democracy. If, by any chance the United States abandons democracy, it is an open question as to how long it will continue in other significant nations. That is why so much of the comment in this text concerns modern democracy in the United States.

In discussing the United States—and democracy in general—I have tried to avoid a common but false comparison. Political characteristics can be meaningfully compared, as can economic characteristics, but there is no value in confusing the two. In the real world, of course, politics and economics are interrelated, and so it is sometimes desirable to discuss both in the same context. One must always be careful, however, to apply the correct labels and specify which aspect or aspects one is discussing. Thus, the correct contrast with democracy is authoritarianism, *not* socialism; the latter refers to an economic system and its correct contrast is with capitalism.

Indeed, discussion of democracy and economic factors is sometimes not only desirable but necessary. Many nations appear to have ignored or abandoned democratic mechanisms and liberties because of what has been perceived as economic—or social—imperatives. The decline of or failure to institute the essentials necessary to insure democratic performance is an observable fact, but it should not be a judgment on the value of different political systems. There are several societies in which democracy is unworkable or is unable to meet the special urgencies of a particular situation. Large, economically underdeveloped nations and small, feudal countries are among those where forced-paced economic progress and social reorganization are necessary. Whether the institution of democratic freedoms would meet their immediate needs is questionable, and many have abandoned them in the immediacy of economic crises. (China, and more recently, Bangladesh, Brazil, Peru, Zaire—the former Belgian Congo—and Zambia provide examples.)

The problem of democracy in many of the Third

World countries may be insoluble. Most of today's functioning democracies achieved the foundations of economic and social modernization before they achieved their democratic political liberties. It was on the distinctly undemocratic base of the Industrial Revolution that modern Western Europe constructed its democratic evolution. The tragedy of the present situation is that the pursuit of economic and social satisfactions in many nations, particularly in Third World regions, is sought within the politico-economic framework of either drastic, enforced populism or coercive and repressive, elite-sponsored free-enterprise systems. In both circumstances, the development toward democratic liberties is not near. These liberties have, it seems, little meaning or worth where physical affluence, mass education, and a prior democratic tradition do not prevail.

Events in India in March 1977 may cause some reflection on this observation. Yet, the Indian situation is probably unique. It is the only modern occasion on which a government with strong authoritarian powers has consciously abandoned those powers, submitted itself to a fully free and democratic test of its popularity, and abided by an adverse result. While India moved to extend and restore democratic practices, several other nations were moving to restrict them. Thailand, Argentina, Brazil, Pakistan, and Bangladesh—all countries with sizable populations and all sharing the economic problems of development—were among those whose forms of government became less democratic than they had recently been. The durability of Indian democracy must also remain in question, for its fragility is already demonstrated.

However, the charisma of democratic terminology or the eventual hope of attaining the democratic vision envelops even those who are either philosophically opposed to it or who are unable to carry it out. An examination of governments around the world reveals that many use the image and language of democracy to describe or perhaps conceal the true nature of their regimes. Several nations calling themselves People's Democratic Republics or Socialist Democracies fall in this category. So do many who pay lip-service to the concepts of democracy while abandoning its reality. Here a careful distinction should be made between democratic socialism and socialist democracy. The former connotes an attempt to blend democratic political forms with distributive economic justice, in such a way as to maintain a largely voluntary relationship between these two elements. In several Western European political systems—notably those of Sweden and other Scandinavian nations—this is the principal direction of state policy. Socialist democracy, by contrast, implies a priority for economics. This neo-Marxian view seeks to substitute public administration for politics. Socialist democracy does not allow for much change in the political or economic order to be initiated through the ballot box.

For many centuries, most thinkers who lived in democracies (and many idealists without) were sure that most peoples of the world would ultimately accept democracy. The early and middle parts of this century encouraged this belief, despite the rise of communism and other authoritarian systems, for decolonization in the years after World War II was potentially a great democratizing movement. The failure of decolonization to produce much democracy in reality plus the evident slippage (if not outright discarding) of the system elsewhere in the world has led to much recent speculation about the future of democracy. Debate frequently takes place on whether democracy is a suitable instrument of government for large numbers of people, whether its success relates to economic or educational levels, whether it will revive or disappear.

Most of these discussions end on a generally pessimistic note and, on balance, the impartial observer would have to agree with this evaluation. It seems to me that democracy is indeed a fading system. The possibility for its revitalization does exist in those few parts of the world that now more or less possess it, but it has little immediate future in the other—and much larger—parts of the globe. However, these conclusions often tend to obscure the central issue in the decline of democracy —the reasons *why* it is in decline. Also of importance are what lessons can be learned from this experience, what tendencies show the most hope of reviving it in at least some nations, and what effects the very existence of democracy has and may have on the future of the rest of the world. It is these features which I have attempted to capture in this series of critical studies.

PART ONE

FUNDAMENTALS OF DEMOCRACY

1   Images of Democracy

Powerful words and phrases evoke strong images on the screen of the human imagination. These mental pictures and associations are often influenced by traditions, cultures, and social conditioning as they enter our consciousness. Locked away between our objective awareness and our subjective perceptions, this imagery awaits only the right stimulus to bring its recall. Depending on the emotional power of the image, that recall can cast an outsized, even unreal projection, which is often mistaken for intellectual truth.

Public opinion research, done in several modern, urbanized societies that have a heritage of western civilization, suggests that the concept of democracy is such an image. It creates positive mental pictures in the minds of most people and projects three assumptions that are closer to illusion than they are to fact. The first of these is that democracy is a good and vital form of government, an ennobling political doctrine, and that many nations can benefit from its application. The United States experience with democracy is universalized and mythologized in support of this assumption. The second image is that of democracy as a system which, over the course of history, has successfully endured long testing and produced a stable political environment. The claim that democracy originated in ancient Greece and the current political condition of Western Europe is presented as fact to reinforce this thinking. The third assumption, particularly deep in the consciousness of the western public, is that most people throughout the world would select democracy as their form of government if they were given a free choice.

These impressions are, in fact, powerful illusions, but

11

they are treated as verified truths and receive wide
sanction in many countries. They thus become important elements in the making of domestic and foreign
policy and profoundly influence the behavior of nations
which see themselves as democracies toward those
whom they perceive as less democratic or nondemocratic. The magnitude of their impact makes each of
these notions deserving of some scrutiny.

There is little historical evidence that democracy is a
more ennobling political doctrine than any other or that
many nations can derive benefits from it. The United
States' experiment is a unique situation and has little
applicability for smaller, less endowed states. Although
it has provided many benefits for those who have lived
within its scope, these are surely benefits which have
come as much from the temperament of its people and
the bounty of nature as from the system of government.
Two hundred years of this system has not had an especially ennobling impact on the character of public life.

There is also an element of unjustified arrogance in
assuming that democracy is the only "good" form of
government available to citizens of any nation. A
"good" government depends on both objective and subjective factors. Obviously, a "good" regime does not engage in widespread torture, in killing of its opponents, or
in violating any other of the generally accepted objective standards of conduct of public affairs. A regime
may, however, be "good" in the eyes of its own people if it
permits or even encourages activities that are censured
by some other peoples. For example, a "good" government might restore polygamy in a culture where this is
considered a useful practice and where a foreign regime
had earlier dispensed with it. The Tanzanian government did this in the early 1970s. Additionally, the people
may consider "good" a government that delivers effective basic services to them, although it may not be
democratic in its character. (Perhaps the People's Republic of China would qualify here.) In short, the evalua-

tion of "good" or "bad" usually has subjective elements that may have little to do with freedom or democracy or "right action" as perceived by others.

The second image of democracy—as a historically tested system and a promoter of stability—seems unverifiable by reference to recorded human experience. While ancient Greece can claim some vague democratic impulses and institutions (Cleisthenes is regarded as the founder of Athenian democracy, c. 508 B.C.), the nature of that society was hardly democratic in any real sense. In the golden age of the city-states of Greece, enlightened Athens had a population of approximately 300,000. However, only about 30,000, or one-tenth of the people, could participate in the election of their rulers or generals or magistrates. Excluded were women, slaves, most non-property holders, and foreign residents. The franchise was restricted only to those of a particular sex, lineage, and economic condition. Only they had a right to vote or to participate in the town-meeting gatherings at which policy was discussed and debated. Solon, the revered lawgiver (638–558 B.C.), Pericles, the statesman (490–429 B.C.), and Demosthenes, the orator-statesman (385–322 B.C.) are among the classic figures of the Athens democratic pantheon. Yet, they were occasional exceptions, whose power derived from a very circumscribed electorate and which lasted for short periods of time. For the most part, Athenian government was not democratic. Dictatorships, tyrannies, and oligarchies, both civilian and military, were the rule. Eventually whatever democratic tendencies existed in Athens were destroyed when the authoritarian state of Sparta defeated Athens in the Peloponnesian War (431–404 B.C.). From then until the twentieth century of our era, the Greeks neither practiced nor extolled democracy.

Antiquity rejected democracy not only in fact, but also in theory. Among the earliest analyses of comparative government are the writings of Plato and Aristotle, the fathers of western philosophy and Athenians who had seen democracy in operation during periods of their lives. After extensive discourses on the nature of society and its organization, both presented democracy as a dangerous and impractical form of political enterprise. Plato advanced the virtues of the philosopher-king and a supportive aristocracy; Aristotle feared that a polity or constitutional government would soon deteriorate into a democracy that demagogues would rapidly convert into a dictatorship. Indeed, he said, democracy would lend itself to tyranny. Looking around their world of the late fifth and fourth centuries B.C., both Plato and Aristotle feared *demos kratia*, the rule of the people. None of their major contemporaries disagreed with them.

Following on Greece, the Roman Republic initially adopted some limited democratic mechanisms, similar to those of the Periclean era. These, too, gave way to the absolutism of emperors. The most famous thinkers of Rome, including Cicero and Seneca, opposed democracy as an unworkable and inferior system. Several centuries later, John Adams voiced their sentiments when he observed, "Democracy never lasts long. It soon wastes, exhausts and murders itself. There was never a democracy yet that did not commit suicide."

For twenty-three centuries after the Athenian experiment with *demos kratia*, few democratic political experiments existed. Monarchies, principalities, oligarchic republics (such as Venice in the fifteenth century), and theocratic states were the preferred forms of political organization. Great civilizational achievements were recorded under such authoritarian regimes. The Renaissance in Europe, the peaks of Chinese, Indian, and Islamic cultures owed nothing to democracy. A few minor exceptions bucked the antidemocratic trend. Several of the North German cities that formed the Hanseatic League in the thirteenth century, a few provincial governments in Swiss cantons, and isolated vil-

lages in India allowed some of their citizens to participate in electing public officials. These were, however,
generally brief, isolated, and uninfluential examples.
The ill-repute of democracy persisted through the Dark
and Middle Ages in the western world.

Political theory of the Renaissance, in the late fifteenth and sixteenth centuries, began to take a different turn. Its major thinkers included Niccolo
Machiavelli in Italy, Jean Bodin in France, and, not
much later, Thomas Hobbes in England. While these
philosophers all unequivocally endorsed absolutism and
saw monarchy as a viable institution, they also began
expanding the concerns of political thought into new
areas. Secular political morality, the nature of law, and
the relationship between the ruler and the governed
were among these. The philosophy of Renaissance
humanism, tending to be skeptical of science and generally indifferent to religion, stressed the importance of
human beings and their supreme value in the universe.
Democracy was not being reborn, but matters close to it
were emerging as some of the major topics of intellectual investigation.

The development of these strands of speculation continued during the period of the Enlightenment in the
late seventeenth and the eighteenth centuries. John
Locke, Jean-Jacques Rousseau, Charles Louis Montesquieu, and others came to repudiate the absolutism of
monarchies and the divine right of sovereigns. The
urgencies that captured their attention were the problems of freedom, of intolerable injustice, of the natural
rights of individuals, of limiting governmental power, of
revolt against arbitrary authority. The era of revolutions was soon to come, and the genesis of modern
liberalism was evolving in the major political and social
ideas of the late eighteenth century.

The era of revolutions did not occur in a political vacuum. While developments in social and philosophic
thought were paving the way for the theories of modern

democracy, the development of several political and governmental mechanisms foreshadowed the forms of modern democratic institutions. Representative local or national legislative assemblies, generally organized as a result of changing economic and political conditions or extending from ancient traditions, were among the most important of these mechanisms. They included the States-General in monarchical France, town councils in North America, and the British Parliament. None of these, however, was truly democratic in the contemporary sense. For example, the British parliamentary system, while having many elements of democratic practice, was heavily influenced by the reigning monarch and was dominated by members of the House of Lords. This nonelected chamber was insulated from public electoral pressure, while the powers of the elected House of Commons were then based on narrow and gerrymandered representation and a very limited franchise. Yet, the presence of these institutions and the increasing sophistication of their approach to government provided a useful preparatory experience. They stood ready to make practical the political and social concepts that philosophic development had evolved.

These concepts drew together a number of political expressions that we now claim to be at the heart of democracy: civil liberties, faith in representative institutions, the rule of law, the rights and the dignity of citizens. The American Revolution, encapsulating these ideals in the Declaration of Independence in 1776 and giving them substance in the Constitution of 1787, was the first large-scale conflict for the realization of these beliefs in a practical form of government. The French Revolution, a much more significant happening for the contemporary world of 1789, further established principles that are recognized today as the roots of modern democracy. (The irony of the nineteenth century was that the American Revolution, little known and not seriously considered when it took place, carried the message of democracy much further than the French Revolution and began to apply it internally. France soon lapsed into a series of dictatorships, which persisted sporadically for almost one hundred years. Its revolution became a symbol for liberty around the world but had little practical meaning for the French or most other Western Europeans until the twentieth century.)

And so we can say, in contrast with popular imagery, that the architecture of democratic government in the way we understand it is of very recent origin and owes little to Grecian antiquity. For most of human experience, democracy has been neither highly regarded nor widely practiced. In fact, it is one of the curious paradoxes of our century that large numbers of people, particularly those in the western world, who articulate the virtues of democracy for their own and other political structures, disavow it in their own immediate sphere of activity. Almost all the major institutions that shape individual lives reject this manner of making decisions or of organization. Most major religious bodies, especially those of the Roman tradition, do not use the democratic method and are convulsed by any attempt to introduce it into their systems. Big business, indeed corporation management at every level, is highly authoritarian. The military, educational institutions, and civil bureaucracies are organized as command operations. Even the affairs of a family, the most elemental unit of human association, are rarely conducted in any democratic way.

Yet democracy's call on the human imagination is so powerful that those who endorse it and those who reject it both make their cause in its name. Believers in democracy or those who see it as part of their worldview frequently make two broad claims for their faith. The first is that democracy exists as a way of political life on this planet. Thus, they refer to democratic governments, generally their own and those for which they have some particular liking, as well as to antidemocratic or nondemocratic states, generally those which they dislike or for which they have had no special affinity. Both these designations are, in fact, inaccurate. Indeed, democracy as a perfected system does not and is not likely to exist. What is labeled as democracy today is more often an aspiration rather than a reality. What does exist are several systems of government that have many elements of democracy and combine these with a commitment to its goals. It is these governments that we designate when we speak of democratic nations in the modern world. Recognition of this difference between aspiration and reality is useful in understanding why nations that we loosely call democratic have so many imperfections inconsistent with the fundamental concepts of democracy.

A second broad assumption that the charismatic image of democracy leads its proponents to make is that most people throughout the world will select this form of government if they have a free choice. This is a highly improbable assertion and is best answered by inverse response. A number of nations have recently abandoned generally democratic forms of government in favor of less democratic mechanisms. Among them have been countries where many elements of democracy have existed for several years and where people have become accustomed to them. India, in 1975, Chile, and the Philippines are among a variety of examples. In none of these cases has there been any major initial resistance to the abandonment of democratic procedures or any popular-based uprising to attempt their restoration. If democracy were so prized a political treasure, the protests would surely have been more vigorous, even if forcibly suppressed.

Another line of this argument concerns countries that have long had Marxist-oriented governments. Militant advocates of democracy persist in claiming that "free choice" would result in the rejection of these regimes and the installation of more democratic structures.

This, too, seems a hope translated into a vision. Although its concentration of state power is immense, the Communist Party of the Soviet Union with its fifteen million members plus the support of its military establishment (assuming all four million troops are fully loyal to the government) could not prevent a nation of 260 million from changing the system if the bulk of the population were determined to do so. Similarly, the thirty-five million members of the Chinese Communist Party, together with three million troops, would scarcely be able to control 950 million Chinese citizens unless there is substantial support for the existing order. The point here is not that these peoples have a free choice of the type of government under which they live: They probably do not. It is that no government of a major nation can sustain itself over a long period unless it has some popular backing or, at least, has a large number of uninterested citizens willing to accept the system. In other words, there may be some or even considerable numbers of dissidents in these countries, but there are just not enough citizens interested in establishing a democratic regime or even in forcing a "free choice."

The concept of a free choice inevitably resulting in a democratic choice has even less validity among the newer nations of Asia, Africa, the Middle East, and the older nations of Latin America. Here traditionally authoritarian methods of governing groups of people have a long history and a high degree of public sanction. In many of these Third World countries, democracy has been a transitional device that has served as a bridge between a colonial era and the authoritarian systems that have replaced it. In fact, these countries seek goals that democracy cannot provide: the immediate recasting of their semifeudal social structures and rapid economic development.

Liberal thinkers once believed that political authoritarianism was a transitory phase that would lead to greater liberty as it matured and evolved. We may now have to consider democracy as a transitory phase between authoritarian periods in the political affairs of most people. This is not to be insensitive to the passing of any freedoms, but to note that excessive expectations, when not realized, lead to rejection of the context from which they do not emerge. These excessive expectations often conceal the historical reality. An examination of the record shows that democracy is a relatively new form of government, with its first major and significant attempt at realization being the establishment of the American Republic in 1789. More often than not, democratic governments have been born from convulsion and have not provided enduring stability. The experience of the United States is not normative; perhaps France under the Fourth Republic (1946–58) and Italy (almost forty governments since 1945) are more typical of the working of modern democratic systems. Democracy, as we understand it today, has not been a particularly effective form of government, except when other conditions, such as economic prosperity, have combined to enhance its capacity. Most people around the world have not been prepared to fight for the establishment of democracy in their nations. In many situations, its replacement by other forms of governance has been received with relative indifference.

Thus, in the modern world, democracy is fast losing out to other political orders, and there is little indication of any mass movement toward the full restoration of democracy where it has been lost or even its revitalization where it exists. It would seem that ours is the declining phase of a brief historical era of about two hundred years. This has been a period in which democratic forms of government suddenly became extraordinarily popular, reaching the high mark in the decade immediately following World War II, only to recede rapidly into the generally authoritarian political condition in which most of humankind has existed and evolved. Even more painful to accept is the idea that this decline has not materially altered the human prospect. The global capacity to feed, procreate, creatively employ, and advance itself has not been substantially affected by the enhancement or diminution of democracy.

This is not to say that the influence of the democratic image is irrelevant to present-day politics. The charisma of democratic terminology carries to those who are philosophically indifferent or ideologically opposed to its vision. Its association with many of the idealistic impulses of human nature, with freedom, justice, and equity, give it a staying power and an attraction. The image is so effective that no regime on the face of this planet can claim that it is against democracy; many authoritarian governments even label themselves "democratic." In that image is the principal strength of democracy, but we must not confuse persisting charisma with growing potency.

2 Democracy as Philosophy

There are two fundamental ways of looking at democracy. In one view, it is a set of methods and procedures for making political decisions and so has little to do with the content of those decisions; it is a process relatively free of any values in itself. Thus, we often hear talk of how democracy is compatible with different economic systems, with one-party, two-party, or multiparty polities, with monarchist or republican forms of government. To perceive democracy in this way is to see it strictly as process, to feel that it can combine with various aspects of other ideologies and so produce a synthesis of a particular political or economic belief with the democratic method. The recent proclamations of Communist parties in Italy and France, the attempts to liberalize Marxism in Czechoslovakia by the Dubcek regime in 1968, and many elements of the Allende system of government in Chile in 1971–73 are essentially efforts toward such synthesis. They seek to establish a Marxist economic order with the use of democratic processes.

This view of democracy as a value-free process tends to ignore a long philosophic tradition; within democracy there have evolved a number of presuppositions and assumptions about the nature of humankind, its character, its aspirations, and its motivations. These core ideas shape a worldview that differs significantly from that of other political conceptions. Democracy then becomes not only a process, but a comprehensive vision of the human purpose and an explanation of the way in which that purpose can best unfold. This perception claims that four fundamental philosophic principles underlie the democratic worldview: freedom, equality, the primacy of reason in human nature, and the distrust of accumulated wealth and power. _____ *what about the prestige attached to wealth?*

Philosophically, democracy also stakes its claim on an optimistic view of humanity. Humanity can improve itself and has the capacity for perfectibility. Given a suitable opportunity, the most positive part of the human character will overcome the negative, and so there is little need to control, guide, or dominate the individual. This contention is a rejection of history and fate, for it resists the idea that external forces, the thrust of events, or the natural and supernatural environment will determine the destiny of the human condition. It is as opposed to the economic determinism of Marxism as it is to the sense of fatalism, resignation, or abandonment to spiritual forces that characterizes several religions. Democracy has faith in the ultimate goodness of the individual and confidence that the collective instincts of the human mass will prove correct. A combination of Enlightenment thinking, Renaissance humanism and eighteenth-century British liberalism underwrite this set of beliefs, but democracy goes further in asserting its optimism under all political circumstances.

—At the heart of this up-beat philosophic construct is the central principle of democracy: freedom. In this sense, freedom is both an intellectual and a social condition. Thought can develop best if it is uncontrolled and *minimal state* citizens can function best if they are least controlled. *ie: Friedman* Freedom embraces a number of liberties, the positive assertion of civil and personal rights, and the implication that government must be as limited as possible. This is the meaning of Rousseau's anguished protest that "man is born free, yet everywhere he is in chains." It is the essence of Voltaire's proclamation: "Those who say that all men are equal speak the greatest truth if they mean that all men have an equal right to liberty." It is the message of the United States' Declaration of

Independence with its claim to the "self-evident" truth that "all men are created equal, that they are endowed by their Creator with certain unalienable rights, that among these are life, liberty and the pursuit of happiness."

Extend this faith in freedom a little further, and it becomes social mobility. One unique feature of early American society was that it sought to replace the social tyranny of aristocracy by an egalitarianism that would reduce class barriers. So important a part of the founding fathers' concept of democracy did this become that it was inserted into the Constitution of the United States. And so the Constitution forbids the granting of any title of nobility and prevents persons holding public office from accepting any title whatever from any foreign source without the express approval of Congress. Here, for the first time in history, was constitutional guarantee that citizens had the right to move upward in society with the same freedom with which they were allowed to earn their living, profess their religion, or select their rulers. Social democracy was to carry the spirit of political freedom.

The U.S. experience also added another new feature to the catalog of freedoms: the freedom to practice the religion of one's choice. Here, too, the absence of any state-prescribed faith was seen as an assurance of liberty to all citizens—a right not present in any significant nation prior to the American Revolution.

However, freedom as the base of a political philosophy presents two self-contradictory propositions. The first was incisively drawn by Henry Grunwald in an essay on the United States Bicentennial.

Our experiments are not often appreciated by the rest of the world, nor are they necessarily comforting even to ourselves. We have broken or bent all the traditional framework of rules: in religion, in family, in sex, in every kind of behavior. Yet we are surprised when the result is both public and personal disorder. We have not grasped the cost accounting of freedom.

The great source of our current bafflement is that we somehow expect a wildly free society to have the stability of a tradition-guided society. We somehow believe that we can simultaneously have, to the fullest, various kinds of freedom: freedom from discipline, but also freedom from crime; freedom from community constraints, but also freedom from smog; freedom from economic controls, but also freedom from the inevitable ups and downs of a largely unhampered economy.

Both American conservatives and liberals are embodiments of this paradox. Liberals are forever asking state intervention in the economy for the sake of social justice, while insisting on hands-off in the private area of morals. Conservatives take the opposite view. They demand self-determination in politics, but suspect self-determination in morals. They demand laissez-faire in business, but hate laissez-faire in behavior. In theory, there is no contradiction between these positions. For freedom to be workable as a political and social system, strong inner controls, a powerful moral compass and sense of values, are needed. In practice, the contradiction is vast. The compass is increasingly hard to read, the values hard to find in a frantically open, mobile, fractioned society. Thus a troubling, paradoxical question: Does freedom destroy the inner disciplines that alone make freedom possible? [*Time*, July 5, 1976]

The second contradictory proposition is one of intellectual and emotional accommodation. Freedom in democracy requires an open toleration and unimpeded expression of many points of view. Some of these may be opposed to democracy itself. Yet it is one of the fundamental liberties of democracy that these views be given equal hearing. This requirement imposes an almost unreal responsibility on individuals in a democratic society. They have to remain convinced of the democratic process, while allowing and even protecting antagonistic opinions. Voltaire encapsulated this paradox: "I disapprove of what you say, but I will defend to the death your right to say it." The tension of maintaining this attitude is evident as democratic forms of government have diminished around the world. It has become axiomatic that, as authoritarianism expands, the first freedom to be reduced is the freedom of expression.

—Another of the central philosophic concepts of democracy concerns equality. Many other worldviews have maintained that inequality is part of the human condition. Some of them, such as Marxism, seek to reverse it forcibly; others, such as fascism, seek to maintain it in the name of a natural order. Democracy holds that all persons may not be equal, but that they have equal rights and entitlements as constituents of a political society. For example, the history of American politics has been in fact a continuing struggle to expand "equal rights" to all citizens. Today the interpretation of this element of the democratic credo is perhaps its most controversial and contested, especially in the United States. Again, to quote Henry Grunwald:

The American promise concerns equality. The Declaration's assertion that "all men are created equal" has always been the most embattled of its "self-evident truths." Philosophers and politicians consistently attacked the idea. "The cornerstone of democracy is a natural inequality, its ideal the selection of the most fit," declared Nicholas Murray Butler. The bitter debate about slavery centered on the belief that neither God nor nature had created men equal in strength or gifts.

But gradually there developed what might be called a respectable American consensus that all people are or should be equal in intrinsic human dignity, equal before the law, and should have equal opportunities in education and employment. We obviously have not lived up to that consensus, though progress has been made toward it. But even as we struggle, more or less sincerely, to improve equality of opportunity, a new and alarming demand is being put forward: the demand for equality of *result*. In brief, this theory holds that natural inequalities of birth, strength, intelligence, and ability are inherently unfair and that justice requires society to compensate for such inequalities. One of the leading proponents of this view is Harvard's John Rawls, who argues in his book *A Theory of Justice* that "equality of opportunity means an equal chance to leave the less fortunate behind in the personal quest for influence and social position." Rawls would allow some inequalities, provided that they benefit the less advantaged members of society. Nevertheless, his views lead logically to the elimination of meritocracy, to quotas in education and other fields, and to drastic redistribution of income.

All this is no longer a matter of theory. The recession and a certain disillusionment with the expensive social remedies of the 1960s may have made us more cautious in what we hope society can accomplish. At the same time, as sociologist Daniel Bell pointed out recently, we are facing a revolution not merely of rising expectations, but of rising entitlements—a staggering increase in the number of things people feel they are entitled to, regardless of their own productivity or contribution to the economy. In the 1960s, says Bell, the government "made a commitment, not only to create a substantial welfare state, *but to redress all social and economic inequalities as well.*" If this course is pursued, it would mean not only permanent inflation, but the disappearance of those incentives that create capital. Or, putting it another way, the shrinking of the very income that is to be redistributed. Above all, it would mean a further expansion of bureaucracy and the power of the state.

This is not an argument against society's providing a floor of safety for everyone, nor a plea against fighting much harder for true equality of opportunity. But carrying equality of results to its logical end would mean the ultimate destruction of the American promise. The ultimate choice is not between equality and inequality, but between different kinds of inequality. Socialism, for instance, promises (on the whole, falsely) economic equality, but in most cases at the price of political equality. In the final analysis, total equality can be enforced only by total tyranny [*Time*, July 14, 1975].

And yet, the belief in "equality" as a natural part of the human heritage survives as a basic ideal of the democratic philosophy.

—Democracy as philosophy embraces reason. The democratic commitment to reason begins with an old premise: People are rational and rationality will eventually prevail over emotion in decisions of public importance. The supremacy of rationality will insure that the average citizenry has the capacity to govern itself and that it will cherish both freedom and equality. The self-restraint, natural discipline, and moderation necessary to operate democracy will flow from reason and logic and will produce government that is both enlightened and harmonious. Group wisdom will enhance this rationality, for democracy maintains that those to whom the people freely give political power may vary in individual intelligence and capabilities, but that, at least over time, their collective judgment will be superior to that of leaders selected in any other way. Winston Churchill abbreviated this concept into the phrase "Trust the people."

Democracy is not so naive as to accept reason as an inherent part of human nature; the history of humankind has too often indicated the contrary. However, the democratic philosophy implies that reason can be learned and so places much emphasis on general education. A well-educated population will have sufficient civic rationality to establish the four basic conditions necessary for the effective working of democracy —restraint on self-interest when it impinges on public interest, resistance to demagoguery and tyranny, development and promotion of high-quality leaders, and acceptance of the obligations as well as the benefits of freedom. That education has proven a feeble instrument in generating these conditions has been indicated with increasing frequency in the twentieth century. Nations with the highest levels of literacy have created the bloodiest wars of our times and of all history. Germany, one of the best educated of states, destroyed its own short-lived democratic Weimar Republic in the early 1930s, accepted the leadership of a tyrannical monster in Hitler, and endorsed both his megalomanic ambitions and insane racial theories. In the United States, which has an expensive and advanced system of public education, voter registration and turnout is consistently disappointing (only 62 percent of those eligible to vote cared to register as voters and only 37 percent of the entire electorate voted in the 1974 congressional elections; 65 percent of eligible voters registered and 53 percent of the entire electorate voted in the presidential elections of 1976). In Britain, a country where literacy is close to total, low polls have also characterized recent general elections.

Thomas Jefferson, together with many founding fathers of the American Republic and other philosophers of democracy, saw the protection of democracy in public education and labored mightily for its expansion: "If a nation expects to be ignorant and free, in a state of civilization, it expects what never was and never will be. No one more sincerely wishes the spread of information among mankind than I do, and none has greater confidence in its effect towards supporting free and good government." His expectations for the impact of learning seem sadly exaggerated when we contrast the worldwide growth of literacy and public instruction with the decline in the forms of democracy and in the number of democratic governments existing today.

—One final principle rounds out the philosophic worldview of democracy. This is a skepticism about, if not a distrust, of money and power and the concentration of authority. Wealth is assumed to have a corrupting influence, and so its holders must be treated with all the equality to which those who do not possess it are entitled. Power and the concentration of authority are equally dangerous; they must be perceived as potential threats to the integrity of government and be diffused whenever they accumulate. Yet the popular political rhetoric of today urges the restoration of trust in government. This statement is antithetical to the spirit of democracy, which is inherently suspicious of government and encourages that distrust as part of that "eternal vigilance" which is the price of freedom.

Here is another paradox that current reality has created. Democracy is skeptical of power, but when all the means to maintain or expand democratic forms fail, it must ultimately rely on power to sustain itself. This is the tragedy of a "democracy" rescued and monitored by the army in Portugal or a militarily policed "democracy" in Greece, Turkey, Pakistan, or Thailand. It is the tragedy of troops enforcing civil rights in the United States or military intervention in public demonstrations in France. Civic consciousness and the other tools of the democratic spirit have, despite long histories, frequently proven ineffective in crisis. Democracy then becomes dependent on what it philosophically abhors—force. There are no regimes today that have sufficient confidence in the strength of the spirit of democracy among their citizenry to abandon the instruments of power as their safeguards of last resort.

This paradox of the use of power in democracy extends to the problem of voluntarism. In both concept and application, democracy espouses a self-motivating style of political participation. Increasingly, this approach has become inadequate to mobilize involvement in the democratic process or to sponsor support for essentially democratic measures. Then more organized, if not almost compulsory, mobilization becomes the alternative to apathy and the perpetuation of injustice. School busing in the United States is perhaps the foremost example of this situaton. When court-ordered and government-enforced measures are necessary to combat public resistence to implementing democratically inspired programs, the voluntary concept of democracy is in danger of negation.

*   *   *

This discussion has attempted to outline some of the components that constitute the spirit of democracy. Most of them are grounded in the idealism characteristic of the late eighteenth century. Modern circumstance has eroded the basis of many of these philosophic premises or made their implementation either difficult or limited. Much of the criticism directed at democratic systems today stresses the loss or neglect of this philosophic basis. Alexander Solzhenitsyn, for one, has denounced western democracy as being devoid of ethical foundation and becoming an empty container in which "parties and classes engage in a conflict of interests, merely interests, and nothing higher." In one of his last writings, in late 1974, Arnold Toynbee warned of the fragility of freedom and the need to encase this essence of democracy in a frame of social stability:

Man is a social animal; mankind cannot survive in anarchy; and if democracy fails to provide stability, it will assuredly be replaced by some socially stabilizing regime, however uncongenial this alternative regime may be. A community that has purchased freedom at the cost of losing stability will find itself constrained to re-purchase stability at the price of sacrificing its freedom. This happened in the Graeco-Roman world; it could happen in our world too if we were to continue to fail to make democratic institutions work. Freedom is expendable; stability is indispensable [*Freedom at Issue*, July-August 1974].

Yet a system that claims to be more than a series of processes must possess a worldview and convey a spirit, however impractical or unachievable that spirit may be in the physical context of a given historical moment. The enduring appeal of philosophy is sustained by its spirit and by its implied ideals, not by the flaws of its analysis and its application. It is on the strength or weakness of these intangibles that democracy competes as an ideology with other powerful (and less democratic or anti-democratic) political concepts of the twentieth century. The acceptance or rejection of this vision and spirit will determine the future of democracy.

3 Men, Institutions, and Beliefs

Men, institutions, and beliefs are three fundamental components of government, and the interaction between them colors the character of governments. The degree of primacy accorded to any one of these elements within a political order determines the nature of that order and the relations between an administration and its citizens. A closer examination of these pivotal centers of political power illumines the meaning of democratic government, especially government in the United States, and helps to clarify the matrix that defines it.

Governments of men are those dominated by or centered on charismatic or dynamic individuals. Charisma merely denotes a special quality of attraction and is neither good nor bad in itself. Hitler and Mussolini used their appeal of personality to establish governments in which institutions were subordinated to their needs and beliefs and were shaped by their personal thinking. Stalin, although not innately a charismatic personality, built the myth of his charisma through total control of the institutions of Soviet government and by bending them to promote his own interpretations of Marxist beliefs. On the better side of the charismatic spectrum, President Franklin Roosevelt projected a personal charisma onto a national environment of economic and strategic emergency and combined power and opportunity to remold the institutions of public administration. A century earlier, President Andrew Jackson, by force of character and capacity to magnetize popular support, had drastically extended the boundaries of executive power. Each of these presidents, however, had an ultimate personal commitment to democratic government, and the strength of U.S. constitutional convictions and institutions acted as a brake on the extremities to which the uses of their charisma might have led them. When there are no such personal or public restraints or circumstances cause restraints to collapse, people dominate governments with little regard to institutions or to beliefs other than their own.

Governments of institutions are those in which the power of a particular organization becomes the dominant feature in the structure of the state. This particular institution develops into the center of national power, and its beliefs tend to become secondary to its organizational needs. As institutions take on a life of their own, the purposes for which they were established are often neglected. The Communist parties of many Eastern European countries are in such a position today. So, also, is Mexico's Institutional Revolutionary Party, born of the first serious social and political revolution of the twentieth century, which has evolved into a major anti-revolutionary establishment. In such cases, the party, its apparatus, and its continuity are the principal concern of public administration, and, indeed, public administration grows out of the party.

An analogy is sometimes made between governments of institutions and the development and organization of the church as an institution in the Roman Christian world. Even though originally founded in order to serve philosophic or spiritual beliefs, strong institutions can come to make their ideals serve them. It then takes an unusually charismatic leader, from inside or outside the system, to break the strength of the institution and restore the primacy of men or of belief. In the Soviet Union, Nikita Khrushchev, during his decade in power (1954–64), attempted this task, but failed to overcome the resistance of the institutional-party loyalists. Unlike Stalin, he was unable to totally dominate the institutions of the state and the party for a long period of

time and entrenched forces, which had been earlier subordinated to Stalin's will, emerged to challenge him.
Khrushchev's efforts finally cost his political life.

In the Roman Catholic church, Pope John XXIII was a
comparable figure. Coming to office, as Khrushchev did,
after the long reign of a powerful, institutionally
oriented leader, John combined the charisma of his person with the authority of his office to impose reform on a
reluctant organization. The Vatican Council, with its
new views on internal church affairs, external policies
promoting better ecumenical relations with other religious groups, and improved connections with the
Marxist world, was the result. These initiatives met
with considerable resistance, but the spiritual source of
papal power assured Pope John of more success than
Khrushchev's secular and institutionally derived authority could bring. The similarity in perspective of
these two remarkable men is startling. Both saw their
principal task as a reforming mission expressed through
policies aimed at curtailing influential institutions that
had become too powerful in themselves. Both used a
high degree of personal charisma in their efforts to restore the primacy of belief, in the case of Pope John, and
personality plus belief, in the case of Khrushchev.

Governments of belief are those in which ideas or
basic concepts take precedence over men or institutions.
Personalities and organizations have to function within
the ground rules that provide the frame of political fun-
damentals. Transgressions are either punished by law
or by public denunciation, and both cults of personality
and potentially powerful and disciplined organizations
are suspect.

China, historically and through the era of Mao Tse-
tung, and the United States provide examples of this
approach. The beliefs of Confucianism determined the
government of traditional China. Its emperor held the
"Mandate of Heaven," the right to rule, because of his
virtue and competence in the Confucian classics. His

personality and the institutions of government were shaped by Confucian belief, and no individual or organization outranked that philosophy.

The doctrine of Maoism occupied this place in the People's Republic of China for almost three decades, since its inception in 1949. Although Mao Tse-tung was among the most charismatic figures of the twentieth century, he consistently stressed the importance of Maoism over the importance of Mao. That is to say, Mao's own perception of his greatness was grounded in his role as the originator of Maoism, rather than in his qualities of personal genius. Thus, the violators of public morality in Mao's China were those who sought personal advancement and promotion of a personal cause or those who sought to advocate the enhancement of institutions at the expense of ideology. China's most serious recent political crises have swirled around these issues. Lin Piao, Mao's heir apparent in the late 1960s, was the principal promoter of the cult of Mao and rose to preeminence on its tide. He also propagated the theory of genius—the importance of individuals (heroes or geniuses) such as Mao Tse-tung in the historical process—and so implied denigration of the role of the masses and of organizations, such as the party, in history. Mixed with these efforts to emphasize personality and charisma was Lin's great enthusiasm for self-advancement. Eventually, Mao and the other leaders of China saw these activities as a threat to their beliefs and themselves, and Lin died in flight from China in September 1971. In the subsequent denunciations of Lin Piao, his apparent rejection of Maoism and the fundamental belief system of the People's Republic has been portrayed as his chief crime.

Liu Shao-ch'i, another potential heir to Mao and then state chairman (president) of China, was publicly repudiated during the Cultural Revolution of 1966–69. His dedication to institutions, both party and executive organizations, had outrun his confidence in Maoism, and his efforts to concentrate the focus of government on them led to his disgrace and removal from office. Here, too, Mao and those closely allied with him demonstrated their attachment to the primacy of belief over institutions. To keep the faith, they were prepared to and did destroy the organization and structure of the Chinese Communist Party. This insistence on correct ideological commitments, in which virtue is associated with belief, remained at the center of the succession controversy in China until the death of Mao in September 1976. Shortly before this event, still another key official, de facto acting Prime Minister Teng Hsiao-p'ing, was driven from public life in early 1976 because his attention to administrative and institutional affairs far exceeded his appreciation of Maoism.

The struggle for power after Mao's death was also a struggle between those who promoted belief in ideas and those who saw the primacy of institutions as more important. After a bitter conflict Mao's widow, Chiang Ch'ing, and her ideologue supporters were swiftly removed from positions of significance and publicly denigrated. The institutional forces of the Communist Party, the government bureaucracy, and the military combined to sustain and expand the authority of the new leader, Chairman Hua Kuo-feng. By early 1977, despite proclamations of ideological continuity, China was clearly moving toward a political system in which institutions would dominate the polity. The next crisis in Chinese politics is likely to center around the possibility that a creature of institutions, such as Chairman Hua, may try to enhance his dominance by converting a government of institutions into a government of personality.

Like Mao's China, the United States also places a maximum priority on belief, although on a different set of beliefs. The belief system on which government of the United States rests is, of course, outlined in the Declaration of Independence and given substance through the Constitution. Sanctity in public office is measured by the degree to which public servants observe constitutional procedures. At the heart of this vision of constitutional government is law and justice, reflected in the aphorism: "Ours is a government of laws, not of men." Although law, in this tradition, is not specifically identified with morality, its violation by public officials casts an aura of immorality on the violators, and this lowers their popular esteem. At the higher levels of government, the loss of this esteem makes participation in political life virtually impossible. To take three widely publicized examples from recent events, President Richard Nixon and Congressmen Wilbur Mills and Wayne Hayes were not defeated in elections, nor have they yet been convicted by any court of law. However, their occupancy of public office terminated because large numbers of people perceived them as having transgressed either law or those beliefs which have become associated with law.

This faith in a set of beliefs, particularly belief in law as the basis of government, has made the U.S. electorate deeply suspicious of the charismatic personality or the highly disciplined organization. Both tend to be seen as potential violators of the law. In the past century, magnetic personalities or military heroes have had few political successes; only the eight Eisenhower years have broken a chain of civilian presidencies. Personality types of the school of William Jennings Bryan, Theodore Roosevelt, or Huey Long, offering drama and charisma as their appeal, have lost many more elections than they have won. Military heroes, such as General Douglas MacArthur, have also been noticeably ignored by the political public. This contrasts markedly with the first one hundred years of the United States' government, when generals occupied the White House for almost one-third of the time, military leaders were frequently

sought as candidates for civic positions, and the revolutionary heroics of several founding fathers paved
their way to the presidency.

This disinclination toward the cult of personality extends itself to political organizations which put loyalty
to themselves above other concerns or which are semi-
clandestine in composition. The inability of the Communist party to make a serious impact, either elector-
ally or socially, parallels the lack of national political
success by groups such as the Ku Klux Klan or the John
Birch Society.

This is not to say that the U.S. tradition is anti-
institutional. However, it makes a careful distinction
between institutions that are part of constitutional
government or are supportive of it, and those institutions or organizations that tend to place themselves
above belief in the law. This is a distinction characteristic of democratic political systems at the present time. A
recent European example perhaps best illustrates this
point. The Communist parties of Italy and France claim
to have abandoned a revolutionary approach to politics
and have embraced the political belief system of democracy. This, they feel, will enable the Italian and French
electorates to view them not as groups that put first
priority on the party (an institution), but as groups that
have subordinated their organization and its Marxist
philosophy to belief in democracy.

With belief in law so basic to U.S. democratic government, does an increase in political or civic law-breaking
denote a decline in democracy? A large number of illegal
activities by major officers and agencies of the state in
vital segments of the social order and by several individuals in public life have recently been uncovered. The
behavior of the Federal Bureau of Investigation, the
Central Intelligence Agency, many large business corporations and labor unions, and several politicians has
been found in violation of the law or is currently under
critical investigation. There are conflicting interpreta-

tions of this phenomenon. One suggests that there is not actually a growth of illegality in public life, but that civic consciousness is more alert. It can, with some truth, be asserted that political corruption was considerably wider in mid-nineteenth century America than it is today. It is only our awareness that has increased. An alternative analysis presents the view that the scope of law-breaking has reached an extraordinary level and penetrated to the highest positions. If the guardians of public morality regularly engage in violating the belief system on which government is based, then this system is in serious trouble. Accordingly, an increase in corruption or crime in civic affairs must evidence a decline of democracy, in faith as well as in fact.

If the latter analysis is correct, there is a dangerous vacuum emerging in U.S. politics. The loss of belief and the resulting decline in democracy are not being offset by leadership or by organizations, both of which now appear to be in a weakened condition. There is no major regeneration of the quality of public leadership, nor is there any major charismatic figure available to enact the system-saving role Franklin Roosevelt played in the 1930s. The possibilities for institutional enhancement are also limited. Membership in political parties is lower than it has been for two decades, public esteem of Congress and the military and the federal bureaucracy is neither high nor increasing, and the general pattern of institutional life in the United States is one of contraction and fragmentation. It is as much a rule of politics as it is of nature that vacuums do not remain unfilled for long periods.

Who and what will fill this developing emptiness? Two possibilities come to mind. The first is that an increasingly enfeebled system will be overthrown and another established in its place. This is an unlikely occurrence in the political and social climate of the United States in the 1970s. A sufficient number of people are satisfied (or not totally dissatisfied) with the nature of American government to prevent such a happening. Although it may be sluggish, the system has not fully lost its capacity to respond, and much is being achieved through its workings. Public pressure, channeled, on the whole, through legal processes, brought an end to the Vietnam War, has extended civil and welfare rights, has advanced the interests of women and minorities, and has caused action on the grievances of youth, environmentalists, consumers, and urban dwellers. It also forced the first resignation of a president and the earlier departure of his vice-president. Such a system is not in danger of collapse.

The second possibility is that renewal will come from within the system as the Roosevelt revival did in the previous generation or the Jeffersonian restoration did at the start of the nineteenth century. It is this possibility which makes the present incumbency of the White House a unique opportunity to preempt crisis. The office of the presidency, by its powers and its morale-building capacity, is ideally suited to engineer such a renewal. If it is unable to do so, speculation on how many ineffective or damaging presidencies the U.S. system of government can survive will not be misplaced.

Hans Morgenthau, one of the pioneers of modern political theory, sees the vacuum created by the decline of democracy as having even more dangerous consequences. He claims this as a sign of a major change in the civilization of politics:

The decline of official government, both in general and in its democratic form, has still another consequence, transcending the confines of politics. In a secular age men all over the world have expected and worked for salvation through the democratic republic or the classless society of socialism rather than through the kingdom of God. Their expectations have been disappointed. The charisma of democracy, with its faith in the rationality and virtue of the masses, has no more survived the historic experience of mass irrationality and the excesses of fascism and of the impotence and corruption of democratic government, than the charisma of Marxism-Leninism has survived the revelations of the true nature of Communist government and the falsity of its eschatological expectations. No new political faith has replaced the ones lost. There exists then a broad and deep vacuum where there was once a firm belief and expectation, presumably derived from rational analysis.

No civilized government that is not founded on such a faith and rational expectation can endure in the long run. This vacuum will either be filled by a new faith carried by new social forces that will create new political institutions and procedures commensurate with the new tasks; or the forces of the status quo threatened with disintegration will use their vast material powers to try to reintegrate society through totalitarian manipulation of the citizens' minds and the terror of physical compulsion. The former alternative permits us at least the hope of preservation and renewal of the spirit of democracy. Neither alternative promises us the renewal of the kind of democratic institutions and procedures whose 200th anniversary we are about to celebrate [*New Republic*, November 9, 1974].

Morgenthau's analysis summarizes the critical nature of the present moment in the history of democracy. Will the behavior and development of politics supply a new faith in democratic belief and strengthen attachment to democratic principles, including faith in the working of law? Or will a continued decline in the forms of democracy move major democratic nations, such as the United States, toward other types of government in which personalities or institutions might dominate the political environment? Glimpses of the answers to these questions can be obtained only through an examination of the workings of modern democracy and the condition of the mechanisms that enable it to function. This is the next area of our investigation.

PART TWO

WORKINGS OF
MODERN DEMOCRACY

4 Definition, Condition, and Mechanism

The philosophic and spiritual vision of modern democracy is encapsulated in writings of the political thinkers of the Enlightenment and those who followed them. Locke, Montesquieu, Rousseau, Bentham, John Stuart Mill, and other visionaries expressed sentiments that collectively created the intellectual heritage of the democratic experience. The conceptual vitality of the seventeenth and eighteenth centuries extended to America. Tom Paine, Thomas Jefferson, and James Madison were among many who provoked American thinking. The Federalist Papers, written by Madison, Alexander Hamilton, and John Jay, contain classic pronouncements of the democratic purpose. It is typical of most constitutional documents that before detailing the mechanisms of government—the institutional and procedural forms—they seek to summarize and give expression to the ideals, such as these, that inspire them. This tendency is particularly present in democratic political environments. Where a system is based on the will of the people, there is a need to explain its goals and state its vision. Three extracts from democratically conceived constitutional instruments are illustrative:

We, the people of the United States, in order to form a more perfect union, establish justice, insure domestic tranquility, provide for the common defense, promote the general welfare, and secure the blessings of liberty to ourselves and our posterity, do ordain and establish this Constitution of the United States of America [Constitution of the United States of America, Preamble, September 17, 1787].

We, the people of India, having solemnly resolved to constitute
India into a sovereign democratic republic and to secure to all
its citizens
    JUSTICE, social, economic and political;
    LIBERTY of thought, expression, belief, faith and worship;
    EQUALITY of status and of opportunity; and to promote
among them all;
    FRATERNITY assuming the dignity of the individual and the
unity of the Nation
... do hereby adopt, enact and give to ourselves this Constitution [Constitution of India, Preamble, November 26, 1949].

We the peoples of the United Nations determined
    to save succeeding generations from the scourge of war,
which twice in our lifetime has brought untold sorrow to mankind, and
    to reaffirm faith in fundamental human rights, in the dig-
nity and worth of the human person, in equal rights of men and
women and of nations large and small, and
    to establish conditions under which justice and respect for
the obligations arising from treaties and other sources of international law can be maintained, and
    to promote social progress and better understanding of life
in larger freedom
... have resolved to combine our efforts to accomplish these
aims [Charter of the United Nations, Preamble, June 26, 1945].

Statements of purpose, however, are given reality
only by the mechanisms through which they are put into
effect. This is generally done through the enactment of a
constitutional document that outlines the basic pattern
of government (although some democratic nations, such
as Britain, do not have a single, formal constitution nor
statement of purpose; rather, they look to a series of
laws and pronouncements to define the powers and
limits of their system). Attempts to define democracy as
a working political system must, therefore, seek to iden-
tify the instruments that are common to democracy and
set it apart from other systems. If we, then, look for
those features that are particular to democracy and

examine their actual operation, we can assess the condition of democracy in nations that so designate themselves.

In searching for these common features, there emerge four broad concepts that democracies claim to accept in theory and realize in fact. They are the practice of representation; the availability of choice and alternatives; preservation of the rights of the individual; and the establishment of public and private security. Each of these is fundamental to the requirements of democracy, and each, within itself, embraces a number of other necessary elements. Taken collectively, they provide the touchstone by which it is possible to test the workings of modern democracy and evaluate the level of its operation.

As we proceed to examine present-day reality in each area, it becomes apparent that the overall pattern of democratic custom and observance has changed substantially in recent times. There is emerging a general weakening in the commitment to and functioning of these procedures in the world at large and a special decline in traditionally democratic societies. This is not to make judgment on the worth of democracy, but to be aware that a major transformation is occurring and that modern democratic systems are evolving away from the concepts and forms that have traditionally been identified with democracy.

*   *   *

The first of these concepts is *representation*. This flows from the belief that citizens can best manage their own public affairs and should do so through participation in the political system. The simplest kind of representation is direct democracy; all qualified people have a voice in an assembly that makes laws for them. This is a method suited to small numbers, such as those who qualified as voters in the ancient Greek city-states or those who could conveniently assemble at a town meeting in eighteenth-century New England. The expansion of the idea of democracy to include larger territorial units, such as the modern nation-state, and larger populations, together with the growing complexity of government, made this type of representation increasingly impractical. And so delegated democracy was grafted on to the earlier form of direct popular participation in government. Elements of this combination could be seen in the evolution of the British parliamentary system beginning in the late seventeenth century, but it was first instituted on a significant scale in the American Republic, when two practices were combined to create the modern notion of representation. These were, first, the institution of regular and unimpeded selection of delegates to a legislative assembly through public election and, second, the exclusive right of the legislative assembly to make laws for those who elected it. Arbitrary and imposed regulation could thus be avoided, and a compromise made between the idea of every citizen as a law-maker and laws promulgated by a small coterie or a single ruler.

There was much controversy over this issue during the early years of the U.S. Constitution, foreshadowing modern disputes about the "imperial presidency." Thomas Jefferson saw the exclusive right of elected representatives to make laws and regulations endangered by presidential authority. He made this a major theme in his victorious campaign against the incumbent president, John Adams, in 1800. A year earlier, Jefferson had charged that

the Federal government, disregarding the limitations of the federal compact, means to exercise powers over us to which we have never assented. . . . The American people and their attachments to those very rights which we are now vindicating will rally with us round the true principles of our federal compact. But determined, were we to be disappointed in this, to sever ourselves from that union which we so much value, rather than give up the right of self-government [Letter to James Madison, August 23, 1799].

Dissolution of the United States was, Jefferson felt, preferable to abridgement of the rights of representation.

The concept of representation raises three allied questions: Who should be represented? What should be the relationship between the majority represented and minorities? How can the high quality of representation be assured?

The right of representation was originally perceived as a limited one, confined to that group in society that was best endowed, intellectually or materially; this led to the establishment of education or property qualifications for the franchise. The reasoning was that an electorate selected in this way would act in the interest of the nation as a whole, that their circumstances would permit them to function as "trustees" for their less competent or less enlightened fellow-citizens. The history of democratic custom is, however, a consistent negation of this elitist view. Over the past two hundred years, there has been a steady expansion of the electoral franchise until it is now essentially coextensive with the adult population in almost every democratic nation. This extension of the right to vote did not come without struggle. In most countries, women, minorities, youth, and the mass of working people were latecomers to the electoral register. Only gradually did the removal of property and educational restriction open the vote to the working class. In 1893, New Zealand was the first country to enfranchise women on equal terms with men, and Australia followed in 1902. U.S. women achieved these rights in 1920, British women in 1928, and French women in 1944. Minorities have had similar problems in gaining enfranchisement or holding public office (for example, until 1858 profession of the Jewish faith was a barrier to membership in the British House of Commons), and many democracies have still not reduced the age of voter eligibility to eighteen from the more traditional age of twenty-one. This was done in the United States only as recently as 1971.

Thus, although it is now practically a norm, the broad, popularly based electorate is a relatively recent development in political history. This does not mean, however, that constitutional government did not exist earlier. In Britain, government has been constitutional, in the sense that it was dependent on the support of a majority of an elected House of Commons, since 1689. Similarly, constitutional government has existed in the United States for two centuries. But it is only in modern times that constitutional government has been linked to the political rights of the bulk of the adult populations in democracies.

Today the concept of representation is threatened in the major democratic nations. This danger comes not from the restriction of the electorate, but from circumvention of its authority. Two sources have contributed to this: the growth of executive power and evasion of the representation process itself. Examples of the former include control of a variety of new regulatory agencies by the executive (as in the United States), monopoly of television and radio broadcasting by the government (as in France), and the growth of executive law through proclamations, executive agreements, and administrative tribunals. Sometimes constitutional instruments unwittingly assist this process. For example, India's constitution permits suspension of state legislatures and the imposition of President's Rule in emergency situations. However, a government with a majority in the national legislature can proclaim an "emergency" of convenience and invoke these special powers. Even during the country's earlier democratic period (prior to mid-1975), several Indian administrations did not hesitate to do so for their political advantage. In 1969–70, almost 25 percent of the Indian electorate was effectively disenfranchised in this way. The twentieth century has been the era of rising executive authority, and each enhancement of it tends to diminish the power of the legislature and thereby of the electorate. This process is not a particularly alarming one in authoritarian regimes, for the nature of political authoritarianism is executive dominance. But its expansion in democratic systems suggests an erosion of the very foundations of democratic government.

The evasion of the electoral process presents another challenge to the concept of representation. Two major democratic systems demonstrate different aspects of this problem. The United States, concerned that its previous method of succession on the death of a president could become troublesome if the vice-president should have to assume the presidency, leaving his own office unfilled for some time (which actually happened after the assassination of President John Kennedy), amended its constitution in 1967 to enable a president to nominate a vice-president whenever a vacancy arises. This would insure that the office of the vice-presidency would not remain empty for long. On the resignation of Vice-President Spiro Agnew in 1973, Gerald Ford became the first vice-president so nominated, and his nomination was duly approved by Congress soon after. On President Richard Nixon's resignation in 1974, Ford automatically became the thirty-eighth chief executive of the United States, although he had been elected neither vice-president nor president. He then nominated Nelson Rockefeller to be his vice-president, and so, between August 1974 and January 1977, the United States government had no elected officers at its head. It can be argued that both vice-presidential nominations were approved by Congress, which represented the people. However, if democracy is a choice among alternatives, Congress was presented with no alternate choices, and the U.S. electorate was not directly consulted. Perhaps the strangest element in this drama was the fact that a president driven from office by public and congressional demands had been able to determine succession to the position he was later forced to vacate.

Another facet of this evasion of the representational process is evident in France, where President Giscard d'Estaing has been largely the political dependent of a force that has long lost a major portion of its public support. The French National Assembly was elected in 1973 for a five-year term. Almost 40 percent of its deputies are members of the Gaullist Union of Democrats for the New Republic, and they worked closely with their then leader, President Georges Pompidou. However, Pompidou died in April 1974, and Giscard d'Estaing, leader of the minority Independent Republic Party, was elected his successor by the French people. Since the Gaullist candidate secured only 15 percent of the vote in this election and was eliminated after the first round in the presidential balloting, it was evident that the Gaullists had lost a substantial degree of public confidence. They still remain, however, the dominant force in the National Assembly and will continue to do so until the next Assembly elections in 1978. This forces President Giscard to negotiate with them on any legislative proposals. In effect, this situation makes both the president of France and its electorate the captives of a party whose performance in several interim political contests indicates a substantial deterioration in its popular position. Although this problem is not unusual in elected assemblies, its persistence for so many years in France suggests that at least part of the spirit of democracy has been evaded through the workings of constitutional institutions themselves.

Evasion is also a device used to maintain an existing political order. To do this, a political establishment excludes from the sharing of power the elements it sees as undesirable for the status quo and so reinforces its monopoly control of the system. By clever manipulation this can often be done through legal means. For example, the Communist Party of France attracted 20 to 25 percent of the French electorate in the past three decades and yet was consistently excluded from participation in government. A similar situation prevailed in Italy during approximately the same period. In these countries two major political forces were effectively disfranchised through a series of political coalitions and maneuvers for almost one-third of the twentieth century. This is a dangerous course for a democracy to follow; it can provoke prolonged frustration and eventual rejection of the entire system by an important segment of the population who may feel that the rules of democracy apply to everyone except themselves. Why play by rules when they are constantly used to your disadvantage by your opponents? The Communist Parties of both France and Italy have, however, made less drastic responses; both in the mid 1970s are seeking government power through understandings with more establishment-oriented forces—in France, through the Socialist-Communist alliance, and, in Italy, through the willingness of the Italian Communists to support and, if necessary, join governments led by others. Many western observers deplore the size, strength, and potentially undemocratic tendencies of these Communists. But we must also recognize their patience with a system that has long denied them a share of power, while rewarding much smaller political groups.

A discussion of representation also raises another current problem—that of majority rule. Reason as the source of political behavior is a basic belief in democracy and this extends to the notion of the conduct of a political majority. Democracy maintains that majorities can and should govern, but that they should accommodate and, if need be, protect the rights of minorities. This thinking was predicated on the assumption that majorities would be strong and sizable. When Rousseau spoke of the general will, he was referring to the Third Estate or "the people" (as against the privileged)—a clear and well-defined majority whose opinion should be reflected in the policies of government. Democracy, in recent years, has witnessed the rise of a troubling phenomenon: It has become harder to get clear majorities. This tendency has been reflected in electoral results. Jimmy Carter was elected president of the United States by barely more than one percent of the popular vote in 1976. John Kennedy in 1960, Richard Nixon in 1968, Harold Wilson in the British general election of February 1974, and Giscard d'Estaing in the French presidential election in 1974 were all elected by majorities of less than one percent. The Labour Party Government elected in Britain in October 1974 received only 39 percent of the total votes cast, which amounted to only 29 percent of those entitled to vote at the election. With this vote, they were able to secure sufficient seats in the House of Commons to form an administration. Most Western European governments are in a minority electoral position and have had to form coalitions in order to rule. In Israel, the Labor Coalition was in a similar situation for several years and the Likud Party government elected in May 1977 has had to resort to the same expedient. The governing Liberal Democratic Party of Japan has not been able to gather more than 48 percent of the popular vote since 1967.

Given the fact that a proportion of any electorate does not vote at any poll, even governments with small majorities find themselves representing only a minority of the enfranchised population. André Malraux points to this as leading to the decline of the legitimacy of democratic governments:

It is a phenomenon of crucial importance for our time because it has only existed since World War II; before then, democratic majorities were significant. Man's historical destiny has diminished to a very feeble point: if the (French) revolutionaries of 1792 had proposed overthrowing the King with a majority of 51 percent, no one would have followed them [*Newsweek*, August 12, 1974].

Governments with slender margins not only find their authority diminished but are also nervous about making important decisions. Political paralysis may result, damaging the entire democratic framework.

Although the narrowness of electoral majorities in democratic nations can inhibit positive government, it can also force a wider consultative process, either with opposition minority groups or with the nation at large. But this, too, can distort the representation process. For example, in August 1976, when Italy formed its thirty-ninth government since the end of World War II, the continued inability of the Christian Democratic Party to obtain an effective parliamentary majority led to it forming a minority government in consultation with a powerful Communist Party minority. Together, these two groups account for a preponderant portion of the Italian electorate. So consultation would seem almost natural. However, in the general election preceding this strange and perhaps temporary accommodation, the majority of Italians had cast their votes for either of these two parties as separate entities, and the result might have been substantially different if they had been aware of what the post-election arrangement would be. Italians had voted for one type of outcome but have since been governed by another type of arrangement, about which they were not asked.

A wider consultative process sometimes comes about when a weak government wishes to evade a legislative battle that it might lose or when it wants to avoid making a hard decision. It then cloaks its weakness in democratic rhetoric and seeks answers to contentious questions in a popular referendum. The British government, for example, used this device on whether to accept renegotiated terms of participation in the European Common Market in 1975. Referendums can play an important part in political decision-making, as with the Italian referendum on divorce in 1974, but there is an increasing tendency to use them as a substitute for effective government.

One of the significant arguments for maintaining an open political system, such as democracy purports to be, is that the concept of representation is based upon and produces a high quality of civic leadership. Democrats claim that domination of political life by a small group or by an elitist organization confines the potential inherent in the citizenry and so retards good government. Thus arises the need to spend public revenues on education in democratic nations, so as to help inform popular political consciousness and develop enlightened leaders from among the people. The processes of representation will be enhanced by the availability of educated candidates for public office and widespread education will strengthen the understanding and the practice of democracy. Historically, the quality of political leadership in democratic systems has appeared to justify these hopes. However, there are two contrary tendencies becoming evident in several modern democratic nations. Both relate to the role of education in political life, and both present complex and potentially troublesome situations for political systems based on the concept of voluntary participation.

Among the best educated democratic nations, such as the United States and Britain, there is emerging an alarming rise in the level of nonvoting. As earlier mentioned, almost 40 percent of the U.S. electorate does not even register to vote. In Britain, electoral turnout has been declining, and even more disappointing is the conscious self-disenfranchisement of British voters—almost 25 percent of those voting in the last national election in 1974 cast their ballots for political parties that they knew could not form a government.

To overcome such apathy, Australia has instituted compulsory voting, with a financial and sometimes a prison penalty for noncompliance, and the use of a preferential type of ballot (in which each candidate has to be voted upon in order of preference; these rankings are taken into account in determining the final result). Belgium also has compulsory voting, but with smaller financial penalties—a system the Netherlands once had and then discontinued because of consistently high voting. This, however, removes the voluntary aspect of representative democracy and eliminates the right *not* to vote. Yet, if electoral turnout continues to decline, these devices may become more common—resulting in the irony of having to nullify an element of democracy to maintain democracy as a whole.

However, there are still many democracies where the level of voting remains high. This is evident in most Western European nations. Voting is also relatively high in India, where almost 70 percent of the population is illiterate. In the 1971 national elections, 55 percent of the electorate voted; in the 1972 election for state legislatures, the turnout was 59 percent; in the 1977 national elections, approximately 65 percent of the eligible voters cast their ballots. (The political paradox of 1971, in which the Congress Party of Prime Minister Indira Gandhi secured 68 percent of the parliamentary seats with only 44 percent of the popular vote, was dramatically reversed six years later. At the controversial national elections in March 1977, the Congress Party received approximately 35 percent of the popular vote and secured only 153 seats, or 28 percent, of the membership in the Lok Sabha [House of the People]. The victorious Janata Party enjoyed the benefit of a much higher level of parliamentary representation than even their winning proportion of the polls justified.)

Another facet of this discussion concerns education and political motivation. Proponents of democratic theory have assumed that education would also lead the most talented segments of a population to participate directly in politics. This was Jefferson's "natural aristocracy," which democracy would nurture, and which would replace the traditional aristocracy of birth or wealth. But something of a reverse process is now taking place: The "natural aristocracy" of our time appears to be withdrawing from political tasks, instead of undertaking them. It is leadership in commerce, science, the arts, education, and the humanitarian professions that attracts outstanding personnel and remains the goal of the most ambitious and enterprising persons. Any judgment about the talent of individuals is necessarily subjective, but there is a wide consensus that the political career now draws less talent than in the past.

Sri Aurobindo, the Indian philosopher and sage, once portrayed the typical politician elected by the democratic process as reflecting the collective weaknesses of his constituents:

He does not represent the soul of a people or its aspirations. What he does usually represent is all the average pettiness, selfishness, egoism, self-deception that is about him, and these he represents well enough, as well as a great deal of mental incompetence and moral conventionality, timidity and pretence. Great issues often come to him for decision, but he does not deal with them greatly; high words and noble ideas are on his lips, but they become rapidly the claptrap of a party. The disease and falsehood of modern political life is patent in every country of the world and only the hypnotized acquiescence of all, even of the intellectual classes, in the great organized sham, cloaks and prolongs the malady.... Yet it is by such minds that the good of all has to be decided, to such hands that it has to be entrusted, to such an agency calling itself the State that the individual is being more and more called upon to give up the government of his activities. As a matter of fact, it is in no way the largest good of all that is thus secured, but a great deal of organized blundering and evil with a certain amount of good which makes for real progress, because Nature moves forward always in the midst of all stumblings and secures her aims in the end more often in spite of man's imperfect mentality than by its means.

If these evaluations are valid, as I believe they are, the concept of representation is in jeopardy and the destruction of democracy is being hastened. Systems led by mediocrities cannot, over a long period, command public respect or loyalty. Eventually the arena of civic affairs is abandoned either to a few activists who manipulate it to their own advantage or to those who call for the overthrow of the existing order. Historically, it can be claimed that more damage has resulted from mediocrity in power and from public apathy than from evil conspiracy.

*   *   *

The second concept that democracies attempt to translate into reality is that of *choice and alternatives*. The theory of choice and alternatives centers on two propositions: that competition in politics helps to develop the quality of civic life and policy; and that the availability of alternatives will prove a check on arbitrary and unchallenged power and assure a responsiveness of power to the opinion of the citizenry. Implicit in this idea is the great construct and true test of modern democracy: the principle of public accountability for those in public positions. As this principle has developed, particularly in the past two centuries, it has been expressed in three major elements of a functioning democratic process: (1) the party system, which gives freedom of organization and intellectual form to differing groups of views; (2) the liberty of expression (from which the current doctrine of the freedom of the press and media has emerged) in order to be able to promote alternatives; (3) the evolution of the role of political opposition, balancing its right to criticize the operation of government with its responsibility not to obstruct the workings of that government. These elements are so important to democracy that they have come to be regarded as basic rights. Safeguarding them is the idea that, in the usual course of events, the organization and expression of opposition are not punishable or treasonable offenses.

The existence of this set of beliefs and rights—and the

degree to which they function effectively—is at the core of democratic government. They are also among the most important features that distinguish democracy from more authoritarian political systems. Of course, there are special situations, such as war or national disaster, during which even the most liberal democracy has to suspend some of its liberties. (Britain and the United States did this during both world wars. However, when the crisis passes, there is a swift restoration of the rights that were temporarily inoperative.)

Non-democracies generally deny one or more of these rights, and the movement of nations away from democracy is usually accompanied by an abridgement of these processes. Marxist-oriented political systems have never had these rights and processes, and, increasingly, a number of democratic nations are slowly abandoning them. On June 26, 1975, the government of India proclaimed a state of national emergency in which press censorship was introduced and the activities of several opposition parties were curtailed. Although there was some reason for these actions, they eroded the Indian claim to have a democratic order. Before the March 1977 elections these restrictions were terminated and their end helped to restore fully democratic political procedures.

Many of those nations that are still practicing democracies are undergoing a fading of the reality of choice and alternatives. This is part of the weakening of the democratic ethos, and it is taking place in a variety of ways, both subtle and overt. The creeping ineffectiveness of political parties is one such indication. In many democratic systems, membership in major political parties is now in decline. This is evident in the United States, in Britain, and in several other European nations. It is accompanied by a self-perpetuating swing in control and orientation that can be described, with only slight oversimplification, as operating in the following way. Control of a political party can go to any of five aspirants: the leader (one person); its senior notables, including its members who belong to the national legislature (several hundred); activists (several thousand); voters (several million); and the paid professional staff, the party organization (a hard core of full-time bureaucrats). If the party's membership is expanding, internal pressures for democratization accelerate, thereby increasing tendencies for the transfer of control from one person or a small group to the groups that represent larger numbers. Attrition of membership, however, makes it easier for a narrow segment to exercise control and to pull the party away from its broadest and most democratic foundations. This is now happening to the U.S. Republican Party, in which a decline in popular affiliation (only about 20 percent of registered voters are now Republicans) has been accompanied by an ideological shift to conservatism. It is also taking place in the Conservative Party in Britain with similar results.

When political parties diminish in membership and in public confidence, the result is usually the growing dominance of one large party, which can maintain its numbers or have them decline at a slower rate than that of its opponents. The effect on the system at large is that a plebiscitarian type of pseudo-democracy begins to replace democratic government. An artificial set of alternatives is then presented to the people. We see this in the United States and Japan today, and it was long the case in India and Italy. The U.S. and Japanese electorates are facing a situation in which almost any Congress and Diet will be dominated by the Democratic Party and the Liberal Democratic Party respectively. Given the rapid decay or growing ineffectiveness of the other major political parties in each nation, these groups have become the "natural" parties of government. The question at elections is not whether a change is possible, but to what degree the voters like or dislike the policies of the existing major party.

Although the legal opportunity to register dissent through elections exists, although the more conspicuous limitations on government power are still observed, and although the forms of democracy persist, the opportunity for genuine choice and possible change has been sharply reduced. Lincoln's vision of democracy —"government of the people, by the people, for the people"—has not yet transcended an older less comprehensive vision—"government with the consent of the governed"; they are deceptively similar, but actually very different concepts of government.

Another factor enters into a consideration of the fading reality of alternatives. The people's lack of genuine choices may not actually have the significance that once attended it. Hans Morgenthau claims that, in many democracies today,

the relevent decisions are made neither by the people at large nor by official government, but by the private governments where effective power rests, and they are made not in deference to democratic procedures but in order to save the economic and social status quo [*New Republic*, November 9, 1974].

The increasing power of pressure groups, including trade unions and large business interests, can make the power of the electorate almost nominal. In Britain, only 48 percent of all employees are unionized. Yet, within the past five years, unions have destroyed one government (the Conservative administration of Prime Minister Edward Heath, in 1973) and held successive Labor administrations to ransom. In the United States, there are several recent examples of business interests corrupting public officials and securing policies or decisions favorable to themselves. The belief that power rests with the people or their elected representatives seems sadly theoretical in these circumstances.

In the United States and a few other countries, there is the healthy counterdevelopment of watchdog organizations, funded by and accountable to the general citizenry. These consumer groups or public-interest lobbies, led by activists such as Ralph Nader or John Gardner of Common Cause, are still in the early years of their existence, but they represent a hopeful source of revitalization for democracy: the public mobilized to expose the excessive impact of special interests. The value of these efforts will depend on their continued impartiality and their ability to focus on *all* special interests with the same degree of effectiveness with which they have scrutinized big business.

The next step for such groups is of particular importance in situations such as the current British context: Once the problem has been identified, what can be done about it? The accumulation of excessive neo-governmental power in the hands of any non-governmental organization (whether it be business, labor, or any other type) betokens an equivalent decline in the power of democratically constituted governments. Part of the problem is the fact that science, technology, and the development of the modern economy have given extraordinary power to those groups that have organized themselves to exploit their political and economic potential. So far, the citizenries of most democratic nations have not been able to organize themselves with sufficient skill to cope with these concentrations of power.

Finally, there remains an issue of transcending importance in the world of modern politics. If democracy does not provide the opportunities for change, if liberties are infringed in the name of democracy, does the right of revolution exist? Many of the great thinkers of democracy have believed that it does. In recent decades, revolution has become more identified with Marxism than with the restoration of democracy. But there is a marked difference between the Marxist perception of revolution and its role as an instrument of democracy. Karl Marx saw revolution as inevitable in the historical evolution of humanity; the destiny of human improvement required revolution and it would, indeed had to, come about. The imperative was primarily economic, although the consequence would be political. What is under discussion here is a different concept: revolution as the mechanism of last resort in correcting the abuses of a democracy gone wrong, revolution as an agency of restoring or enhancing democracy itself. Economics may or may not be involved; the prime motive is political and philosophic.

American revolutionaries claimed and exercised this right of revolution two hundred years ago. Lincoln, in his first inaugural address in 1861, used the cadences of contemporary radicalism to discuss this matter. "This country, with its institutions, belongs to the people who inhabit it. Whenever they shall grow weary of the existing government, they can exercise their *constitutional* right of amending it or their *revolutionary* right to dismember or overthrow it." In various writings, Jefferson, Madison, and others agreed that revolution is a right of the citizens of a democratic nation. However, many democratic constitutions do not extend that privilege to the people and charge the government, implicitly or explicitly, with the obligation to suppress rebellion. The right of revolution is, indeed, accorded to citizens in the constitutions of several states in the American Union; the Federal Constitution, however, does not specifically designate it as a constitutional right and is unclear about its existence. At what point, then, does revolution become a legitimate recourse, and is this a right that can be vested in the hands of a few "representatives," so that they can act on behalf of the people? Modern radicalism, in its most idealistic form, seeks to reverse the complete identification of revolution and Marxism and to present the alternative of democratic revolution to the people. Perhaps we should remember its message whenever we feel uncomfortable with its form; for political liberty within society is best measured by the level of unorthodoxy which that society tolerates.

handwritten margin note: → then the American's blind hatred of socialists proves the extent of their political liberty.

* * *

A third concept that concerns the definition, condition, and mechanisms of democracy is that of the *rights of the person*. The theory of modern democracy maintains that there are possessions that inherently belong to each individual and cannot properly be transferred or be abridged by law; like each citizen's heart, they are the irreducible birthright of every human being. These include freedoms of speech, of assembly, of the vote, of thought, the freedom from arbitrary arrest in law and other liberties of the person. Here also is the freedom of religious belief, a daring innovation when introduced by the U.S. Constitution into the eighteenth-century world. (The word "God" does not appear in the Constitution; in forbidding the establishment of a state or national religion, the U.S. Bill of Rights decreed, on the federal level, a separation of church and state.)

Some of these rights or freedoms go back to the Magna Carta, concessions that the barons seized from King John of England in 1215; some have their source in Anglo-Saxon common law; some have evolved from more recent democratic custom; some are identified as fundamental human rights in legal or constitutional documents in several nations. In most democratic systems, these liberties are protected by a process of independent judicial review by which individuals can challenge, restrain, and redress their impingement. The agglomeration of these rights, and the ways in which they are preserved, define many of the practices of democracy. At the center of all of them is the concept of the freedom of the individual person.

Modern society balances these rights of the person with the collective rights of society as a whole. The latter include commitments of society to provide freedom from want, freedom from fear, freedom from economic insecurity. Some of these rights are as old as the organization of human communities; some were articulated by Karl Marx. Several were proclaimed by President Franklin Roosevelt in his "Four Freedoms" speech in January 1941, and, in August of that year, inserted into the Atlantic Charter, which he and Winston Churchill issued and which was subsequently endorsed by all the Allies fighting Germany in World War II. Much social progress in the twentieth century has come from the recognition of the existence of these collective freedoms that government action can establish for all citizens within a nation. Both democratic and non-democratic governments frequently frame state policy around these collective rights. Economic security for everyone in society—elimination of the fears of unemployment, impoverishment through illness, inadequate protection in old age—is one of their vital components.

There are, then, two broad conceptions of personal rights. The older democratic vision is grounded in the rights of the individual; the other, a more recent response to the concern with society as a unit, is grounded in the collective rights of society. Theoretically the different conceptions do not contradict each other, but, as they are translated into practice, the demands of the two often clash. The rights of the person may have to give way to collective rights, or the reverse may be required, in order to achieve progress in one area or the other. In an earlier period, the focus of democratic systems was primarily on individual rights. More recently, under pressure for social justice, the stress has shifted toward collective freedoms. In that process, several personal liberties have become somewhat restricted in the interest of society as a whole.

A modern example underlines this point. The incidence of terrorism has made it necessary for many nations to treat each air traveler as a potential terrorist. Our personal rights are infringed as the normal legal assumption of innocence until proven guilty is abandoned when we are both arbitrarily searched and delayed before we board an aircraft. The collective freedom of society—the need to be free from fear—has achieved primacy over the freedom of the person. Terrorism is, of course, an extreme situation. But what if the rise in urban crime eventually leads to a situation where all those who use public transport have to undergo a physical search before they are allowed admission? An initial and tolerable violation of personal liberties for the collective benefit of society can become an assault on basic democratic rights in the name of protecting society.

Another aspect of this conflict between personal and collective liberties concerns property. Ownership of property has long been a cherished right of the individual citizen in a democracy. Almost every constitution in a democratic political system guarantees this right, and where a formal constitution does not exist, as in Britain, the basic laws of the nation provide this security. However, property ownership is increasingly under attack in many modern societies as the ethic of distribution tends to supersede that of accumulation. Marxist governments achieved this in a drastic way at the inception of their regimes; democracies are slowly moving in the same direction under the pressure of social theory and economic needs of the masses. As this trend continues, limitations on the ownership of property may make this right an obsolete relic of a more affluent age.

In these and many lesser ways, democratic systems are today subordinating the rights of the person to the collective rights of the community. These inroads may be justified by the circumstances of modern existence. However, to the extent that democracy has been built on the liberties of the individual, such subordination reflects a weakening of one of its key supports. What is needed, then, is not necessarily a return to the concept of the inviolability of personal rights, but an attempt to reconcile the needs of those two sets of rights of the individual and to define the combination in which they can harmonize personal liberties and social requirements. Few nations have addressed themselves to this problem in the context of preserving modern democracy. This is particularly true of many of the newer nations in the world, where the collective interest has been, at least theoretically, pursued, and the framework of democracy badly damaged in doing so.

*   *   *

The fourth concept that generally identifies a democracy relates to *public and private security*. There are many strands that weave into this concept, but three are of immediate importance to the operation of democratic government today: protection of the citizenry; restraint in the use of the means of coercion; and both protection and restraint in the area of external or non-domestic pressures. Within any society, governments have the sole legitimate monopoly of the means of force. It is only they, or those to whom they grant permission, who have the legal right to use this force on anyone else. Democracy assumes that this power will be used with restraint and to provide protection for the people. However, there is a paradox in giving a man a gun and telling him that he is the only person who can legally use arms, but that his weapon should be used exclusively to protect others, including those who oppose him, and not to extend his own power. To reject the temptation to promote self-interest requires superhuman restraints; many have fallen prey to its seductive propensities, preferring to abandon the principles of democracy and use their command of physical force to protect themselves or punish those who might threaten their position.

Constitutional democracies have sought to offset the temptations inherent in possession of the instruments of physical coercion with legal safeguards for the rights of the individual. Thus, the Constitution of the United States entrusts its government with the power to maintain domestic tranquility, common defense, and the establishment of justice. The second, third, and fourth amendments to the Constitution, however, counter these powers with provisions that favor individuals in order to shield them from the military, police, or security forces of the state. Yet governments cannot exist without this power. The safety and protection of all citizens and the establishment of public order are paramount conditions of modern society. An administration that cannot assure physical security within its territory does not fulfill the most basic function of government and will gradually lose its capacity for effectiveness in other areas.

This is one of the growing incapacities of modern democracies. It can be argued that public order has recently been maintained in parts of Britain by those who break the law and not by those who are responsible for enforcing it. Whenever the terrorist factions of the Irish Republican Army wish to disrupt British life they have been able to do so with relative ease, and the guardians of the law seem unable to prevent it. In many other democratic nations, the degree of lawlessness is increasingly dependent on the energy of criminals rather than on the effectiveness of crime prevention agencies, such as the police. The helplessness of publicly funded efforts then leads to the expansion of privately funded protection services, including security guards, vigilante groups, and detective organizations. These incipient private armies will, if the need for them continues to develop, pose a potential threat to democracy itself.

In the alternative, public outrage and demands for personal safety by the citizenry can produce an atmosphere in which demagoguery can flourish and democracy be abandoned. The Federal (Weimar) Republic of Germany, established at the end of World War I, was destroyed in just such circumstances by Adolf Hitler. Hear his campaign rhetoric in 1932, the year before he achieved governmental power:

Sounds like U.S. Congress rhetoric.

> The streets of our country are in turmoil. The universities are filled with students rebelling and rioting. Communists are seeking to destroy our country. Russia is threatening us with her might, and the republic is in danger. Yes, danger from within and without. We need law and order.

Remember, too, that Hitler came to office through democratic elections in which the bulk of the German people responded to this appeal and its hope for order out of chaos. They were prepared to accept a little less democracy for a more secure social condition. The outcome was national and global horror.

The problems of security within a democracy are not restricted to the dangers of ineffective or overzealous police forces. When the normal mechanisms needed to make democracy work are threatened, internally or externally, governments look to the military to provide the last line of defense. During World War I and World War II, for example, they performed these duties against external aggressors and so preserved democratic society in Western Europe and North America. On other occasions, they have also helped maintain and protect the democratic system. But today a number of social and political factors have made the military's loyalty to the system questionable in several democratic nations. France and the United States provide two current examples. In December 1974 the French chief of staff, General Boissieu, compiled a confidential report on army morale. His judgment, as later revealed in the newspaper *Le Monde*, was that the military was unreliable in domestic crisis. If another period of civic disturbance, such as that which shook France in May 1968, were to occur, unrest might spread to the army.

The United States has a serious potential problem

with its army, which switched from drafted to fully volunteer recruitment in mid-1973. In times of inflation, economic recession, and high unemployment, minorities are generally hardest hit. Many of them then seek enlistment in the military, an avenue of sure employment with opportunities for advancement. Black Americans, who represent 11 percent of the population, currently number around 20 percent of the armed forces' total manpower. In units that would be directly involved in combat, the marines and the army's ground forces, the average proportion of blacks will soon be over 35 percent and is likely to go even higher because of their heavy re-enlistment level in the lower ranks of the army. Can armed forces, unrepresentative of the society they are expected to serve, be depended upon to fight for the preservation of a status quo that has seriously disadvantaged them and those closest to them? If U.S. democracy is ever desperately endangered, its defense will be largely in the hands of those who have least benefited from it. The United States is not alone in needing to face the social and political implications of the composition of the modern military; the problem extends to several other democratic nations.

The concept of protection from and restraint in the use of the agencies of force relates to another important question. What tactics are appropriate for a democracy to use in implementing its foreign policy? The growth and activities of the clandestine agencies of government, especially such institutions as the Central Intelligence Agency in the United States, bring this issue into focus and provoke two conflicting views. There are those who believe that like has to be countered with like, and that the conduct of an effective foreign policy requires a response to the methods used by one's global rivals. Thus, if the Soviet Committee on State Security (KGB) resorts to subterfuge, covert intervention, deceit, and even assassination, democratic intelligence services must react in kind. To do otherwise would be to place the international community at the mercy of its most ruthless members and even endanger democracy itself. Others feel that the division between constitutionalism and legal processes at home and "illegal" behavior abroad is a very thin line of distinction, and the infection of authorized illegality in one area will inevitably infect the other. Watergate, in this perception, was the logical result of various abandonments of lawful methods in the execution of foreign policy that eventually spilled over into domestic politics. In this view, the spirit of democracy requires that indignation at the violation of the rights of citizens should not be confined to violations in one's own country. (In early 1977, the newly elected Carter administration frequently articulated this sentiment in its declarations on U.S. foreign policy.) The latter opinion is idealistic, but it is also much more in keeping with the traditional concept of democratic procedures. Yet the prevalence of the former view and the actions it is used to justify indicate the extent to which the erosion of the democratic method has taken place in the conduct of foreign affairs. Nations, like individuals, cannot have two personalities without the characteristics of one affecting the environment of the other.

In a major way, this problem arises from the advancing interdependence of the present-day world. When democracy was conceived, public affairs could generally be clearly divided into those concerning foreign and those concerning domestic matters. As modern government has evolved, the democratization of domestic policy has received much attention. Foreign policy has been largely left, until very recently, to the executive agencies of government. The immediate priorities of the electorate, the executive's superior access to diplomatic information, and the lack of knowledge of foreign affairs on the part of the elected representatives of the people have contributed to this neglect. However, the understanding that international relations now have serious domestic consequences has rapidly changed this attitude and is beginning to produce a democratization in foreign-policy making and execution. This, of course, is strongly resisted by executive officers of several democratic governments—the reluctance of former Secretary of State Henry Kissinger to encourage Congressional participation in or scrutiny of foreign policy being a typical response. What we are witnessing today is the gradual breaking down of the classic divisions between internal and external affairs and the growing recognition that no government—democratic or otherwise—can be insensitive to the influences of external pressures. The issue of security, which we examined from the viewpoint of internal threats to the citizen, now frequently reaches to the nation as a whole, and the source of threats to security can often be located outside the country.

*   *   *

We have presented four of the major concepts of democracy and the ways in which they have been translated into reality in the major democratic nations of the world. In that they are still working parts of the political process in most of these nations, it can be claimed that the condition of democracy has considerable vitality. However, the ways in which these concepts are practiced and the increasing erosion they have suffered in recent years must lead to the conclusion that several of the institutions of democracy are in decline. There is, it seems to me, little possibility for a large scale revival at hand. The regenerative mechanisms, which offer hope for the future, are discussed in the last essay in this book. However, I do not believe that they are sufficiently effective to restore the traditional forms of democracy. In this context, it is perhaps appropriate to focus now on whether the present condition of democracy is caused by its internal functioning and whether this condition will lead to a new system of "democracy" or to its rejection.

5 Overload and Oversell

In its workings, modern democracy is both a function and a motivating process. The functional elements encompass a complex of interlinked administrative activities: those concerning the operations of government as a mechanism for policy implementation and as a vehicle for delivering services to the people. The motivating process elements relate to the political system and its capacity to mobilize people, inspire their participation, and secure their confidence. Among the most important of democratic countries, at the present time, the working of these two aspects of democracy appears to be under considerable strain. These are symptoms of a fatigue which comes, not from a conceptual disorder, but from reality trying to measure up to excessive demands and expectations.

As a function, democracy suffers from a heavy overload. This is largely the result of its own success in modern times. Those democratic nations in which the system has existed for a considerable period have been able to create three extraordinary conditions: a consistent increase in the output of wealth, a rapid growth in the numbers of educated people, and an effective expansion of the role of government in society. Despite two world wars and almost a decade of severe economic depression, this trend was maintained during most of the early- and mid-twentieth century. But, it contained within itself many of the perplexities that have surfaced more recently. The results of wide public education are perhaps most responsible for this, for its advancement has quite naturally led to growth in the expectations and hence demands of increasingly larger groups of citizens. Initially, these demands were expressed in fairly simple terms, which were not too difficult to satisfy. Among these were political rights, basic public services, and some forms of economic regulations, such as the imposition of taxes or controls on rapacious entrepreneurs or the establishment of decent work and wage conditions.

Each of these measures brought greater intervention by the agencies of government. And the relative effectiveness with which they began to administer a wider range of activities did instill confidence in the functional capacities of government. But the satisfaction of many basic demands gradually led to escalated sophistication. Rising expectations dovetailed into rising entitlements, and, as sociologist Daniel Bell analyzes the phenomena, this was accompanied by a belief that government could redress almost all social and economic inequalities. A changed perception of wealth confirmed this belief. Masses of better educated people began to see that democracies were very good at producing wealth, but much less capable of distributing it. They began to understand not only that things were inequitably shared in society, but *why* these inequities existed and how they could best be corrected. Government and its operations were the only instruments which were both available to large segments of the people and capable of delivering these adjustments with relative speed. The insistence that government accept this responsibility was pressed by two important social forces: by the large number of underprivileged who would benefit from these actions and by the liberal reformists who saw this as a method that was socially enlightened or that was capable of preserving a system which might be endangered by the violence of the frustrated underprivileged.

So government became the organ of national self-improvement and reform. And indeed, contrary to the mood of current popular belief in many democratic nations, government did begin to perform major new tasks of an economic and social nature with reasonable competence. In the United States, these included the extension of social welfare, the policing of minority rights and of minority improvement programs, and the initiation of nationwide efforts to provide unemployment and medical benefits. In Britain, the establishment of a national health system and the nationalization of critical industries were accomplished through the functional activities of government. In most Western European nations, the adoption of similar programs brought vastly improved conditions of life to the least affluent of their peoples.

Unfortunately, government, which proved so effective at initiating these developments, has proved a poor continuing manager of its expanded functions. Students of management theory suggest that an increase in workload leads to two developments: increased bureaucratization and increased budgets. In almost every democratic nation, a functional overload has produced this result, adding to government bureaucracy and budgets. However, unlike business corporations, where the presence of profit and production necessities check inefficiencies, governments have not improved their competence by the expansion of personnel and financing. While the proportion of government spending to national income has burgeoned and the power of government institutions has grown almost as rapidly, its capacity to manage a variety of expanded functions has either declined or, at best, not improved.

The United States provides a typical example. The scope of government services and functions has increased dramatically in the past two generations, and this is reflected in both spending and employment. In 1929, total government expenditures (federal, state, and local; military and civilian) accounted for 12 percent of the national income; by 1973 it had risen to 39 percent. At the present time, government provides employment for around 15 percent of the total labor force, a higher figure than in any other peace-time period. Yet, the single most potent political slogan of recent years has been that of "over-bureaucratization," reflecting deep dissatisfaction with the operations of government. In Britain, where almost one-half of national income now flows through the public sector of the economy, a similar disenchantment exists. In many Western European nations, Canada, and Australia, antagonists of bureaucratic expansion have made it a fierce and successful election issue. Given the popularity of this sentiment, a significant attempt to scale down the functions of government and improve its operational performance is likely to soon take place in many nations.

The overload that has produced this result is, as we mentioned, the product of a democratizing process in older democratic nations. The inability of government to cope with this load has placed pressure on all government institutions in two ways. First, it makes government appear ineffective and produces a crisis of authority. French sociologist Michel Crozier sees this as a real threat to western democracies and a significant contributor to the rise of the Communist Parties of France and Italy.

The challenge doesn't come from the Communist vote as such; the challenge comes from the incapacity of Western democracy to govern.

It also comes from the decay of institutions such as the church, education, the army and, to some extent, the bureaucracy. All this is at a time when one institution has not yet decayed: the Communist Party.

I don't believe the Communist Party has provided a real appeal. In Italy, the appeal is not of Communism of the traditionally ideological kind, but social democracy. But the Communists win because people are so disgusted with the prevailing chaos and because the Communists are honest and efficient administrators. The problem in both countries is that the Communist Party has an organization which operates efficiently: When someone takes a decision, it's obeyed right down the line. This is about the only organization where this is still happening. In most other organizations, people are unable to take a decision—or, when it is taken, it's not obeyed.

The superiority of the Italian Communist Party is very impressive. It doesn't work that well, but it works so much better than the other parties and the bureaucracy [*U.S. News & World Report*, March 8, 1976].

The second consequence of the functional overload is that it weakens public faith in democracy and ties functional incompetence to conceptual inadequacy. This is an unfair connection, for democratic government was not conceived as a managerial institution for all public social and economic agencies. Yet, the link persists in the minds of many. These emotions have provoked the paradox of a current clamor for "limited government," while not reducing public demands on government. Perhaps the application of this policy will restore a realistic popular appreciation of the relationship between the managerial tasks of bureaucracy and democracy as a political system.

If overload has impaired the workings of democracy as a function, oversell has impaired its credibility as a motivating process. There is a cynicism at the pledges of politicians and a serious crisis of belief in the integrity of democracy. Richard Gardner, of Columbia University, explains: "The problem is not only conceptual, it is political. The world's political systems, whether democratic or totalitarian, reward leaders for maximizing present benefits to their people while passing on the costs to other countries, to future generations and to mother nature." Gardner might have added that democracy, more than other systems, encourages this tendency. Authoritarian leaders have much less need to court public favor, since they are not subject to regular elections and can suppress media criticism.

Faith in political promises has not been enhanced by the policies of politicians in many democratic nations. As the stakes increase and the competition grows more vigorous, the promises made by political leaders seem to escalate. The Labor Government in Britain came to power in 1974 on a platform that rejected wage and price controls. Less than one year after taking office, they hastily instituted these controls. This closely parallels the behavior of Canadian Prime Minister Pierre Trudeau during approximately the same period.

Although crises often have to be met with flexibility, the contrast between promises made to be kept and promises made for electoral expediency distinguishes a statesman from a politician. Why, then, does not the voter make this distinction and vote for the statesman? The answer is that there may not be that choice. The *Economist* newsmagazine summarized this dilemma:

The nature of the burgeoning "crisis of democracy" is that while the ballot box is the best way of choosing a man or team to make the great decisions as between peace and war, or as between hard-heartedness and compassion, it is now proving one of the worst ways of choosing who shall spend more than about 10% of our money or of deciding who shall boss our lives. If we yield too much power to bodies that are elected (for example, governments and trade unions) then an undue influence will be wielded over us by even the most inefficient and extremist of the 2% who want to participate in public affairs; this is a deprivation from the freedom of the 98% of us who just want to be discriminating and choosey consumers of good government like we are discriminating and choosey consumers of good soapsuds. The *pons asinorum* of modern politics is to realize that even the poorest housewives are getting a better choice of soapsuds (by buying them in supermarkets) than they are getting of politicians (between, say Nixon or McGovern or Wilson or Thatcher at the ballot box).

One way out over the next few decades, so as to return power to the 98% and also to bring back efficiency, will have to be to cut sharply the proportion of gross national product spent by governments, and to return a lot of present public services to rule by the marketplace. Much of the battle will be to break through the resistance of the vested interests which have gained in *amour propre* while the 2% of the bossy have grabbed too much power from the 98% of the intelligently uninvolved [December 6, 1975].

The oversell of those who participate in democratic politics clearly reflects lack of high-quality leadership; therefore, one solution to the problem may lie in education of political leaders. Politics is perhaps the last major profession in which totally unqualified persons can present themselves for a position and, if selected, pursue a career. It might be a theoretical diminution of democracy, but a likely improvement in its practice, to require that all who make a career of politics undergo some form of training for government, at public expense. This would not be an easy proposal to implement, but it offers a possibility of restoring the credibility of democracy and effectiveness in its workings.

There is a certain poignancy to the deep-seated unhappiness with the workings of democracy in Western Europe and North America. The many condemnations of it are not matched by much intellectual creativity. There are no significant alternatives to democracy that enjoy widespread appeal or have had even minor successes. During the Great Depression of the 1930s, another period of crisis, several other models of government captured the public imagination. Fascism, communism, and extreme solutions of the political right or left became fashionable. Democracy was barely able to withstand their challenge and, indeed, failed to do so in several European nations. Since World War II, despite its paradoxes and problems, democracy retains its hold on the public imagination and no other political system has been accepted by the free and unimpeded choice of the people. Today, Communist parties, Southern European nations emerging from long years of authoritarian rule, and weakening European democracies all proclaim their dedication to democratic methods and procedures. The sincerity of these claims will soon be revealed by the level of their commitment to improve the workings of democracy.

6 Economics, Democracy, and the Global Village

History tells us that two seminal events took shape around 1775. The Industrial Revolution gave birth to modern, urban society in Britain, and the ideals of modern democratic government found expression in the beginning of the American Revolution. The close timing of these events was largely coincidental. The onset of industrialization and modern capitalism had little to do, directly, with the urge for independence in the American colonies. However, for most of the past two centuries, there has been a close linkage between industrial society and the process of democratic politics, and of both to the British and American experience. The record of this experience is one of gradual integration between industry and democracy, industrialization initially coming from Europe to America and democracy expanding the other way, until the term "modern industrial democracy" has come to describe most North Atlantic nations.

From an analysis of the social histories of these countries came three propositions that were long considered fundamental to the concept of modern society:

1. That democratic political forms are an integral part of the character of modern society and reinforce its durability.

2. That the expansion of modern society would lead to the expansion of democratic government in the world.

3. That modern society was the fastest agency for creating wealth on a national scale, that it would lead to global economic leadership, and that it could create

communities where private profit and public good could coexist and be mutually supportive.

In the nineteenth and earlier part of the twentieth centuries these assumptions were apparently validated by developments in Europe and America. Levels of affluence, industrialization, and democracy all advanced within the economic framework of capitalism. Modernization under authoritarian systems, such as that which occurred in Germany and Japan, ended in the destruction of both these systems and their economic achievements. As a result, much credibility attached to the notion that modernization would not occur unless accompanied by democracy. By extension, it was argued that democracy could be an effective means of developing economically backward areas of the world.

The definition of a modern society expanded to incorporate these beliefs. Originally, modern society was viewed largely as an economic entity, with urbanized industry and technology at its foundation. In the early twentieth century, the ideas of social modernization began to extend to public life, embracing a variety of additional elements—the ethic of social welfare, opportunities for mobility, and a sense of judicial and political egalitarianism. This new perception began to graft a series of democratizing visions on to the traditional economic dimensions of modernization.

In the past decade or two, this conceptual confluence has begun to fragment. The characteristics of modern society are increasingly evident outside its focus in North America and Europe. As this geographic outreach takes place, all three of the "basic" assumptions about modernization are proving false or irrelevant in other regions. Many developments give witness to this fact. For the first time in its history, modernized society is being separated from democratic political forms. Rapid and lasting modernization is evident in a number of Marxist and authoritarian systems, suggesting that it can evolve without a concomitant commitment to democracy. At the same time, we have seen that genuine forms of democracy can endure in nations that have not modernized; the Indian experience underlines this development. (Interestingly, the constriction of democracy in India between 1975 and 1977 was accompanied by signs of accelerated economic and social development efforts, and a major test of the newly elected government will be its ability to maintain this progress in the context of a revived democratic polity.) The swift economic gains of many oil-producing countries within the past five years show that neither democracy nor modernization is necessary to gain international economic leadership and that a fast route to such prominence can include the possession and effective management of scarce natural resources. Finally, the ability of private profit and public good to coexist is in question, even in some of the traditional industrial democracies.

As modernization begins to expand, democracy is losing its vitality as a national political process. This decline is an observable fact throughout the world today. In Asia, the Middle East, and Latin America, many regimes describe themselves as democracies, but only a handful maintain the basic conditions of that reality. There are almost fifty nations in Africa, but only one (the Republic of Gambia—among the smallest and least important) has a serious claim to the type of political system we have defined as truly democratic. In Eastern Europe, the Marxist-oriented states are essentially one-party governments. Many newer nations which have practiced democracy at various times in their existence have abandoned it in the past decade or so. While the trend has flowed strongly toward authoritarianism and the modification or curtailment of democracy, very few nations have moved away from authoritarianism toward democracy in the past ten years—Greece and Portugal since 1974, and Spain since the death of Caudillo Francisco Franco in late 1975. Democracy was restored in Thailand in 1973, but it was terminated three years later when the military dismissed the elected government and replaced it with surrogates of their choice. In none of these nations is democracy secure or deeply rooted as yet; where it exists, it is a frail and tentative implant.

India appears to counter this anti-democratic trend. After almost two years of expanding authoritarian government, Prime Minister Indira Gandhi decided to have democratic elections in March 1977. These elections were conducted in an open and unimpeded way and the authoritarian measures previously imposed were suspended for this purpose. The electorate rejected Mrs. Gandhi and her Congress Party and gave a resounding victory to the opposition Janata Party. Many political analysts claimed this as a major advance for democracy and a signal that even a poor nation will place political liberties above economic priorities. This, it seems to me, is a relatively simplistic perception; the electoral issue of freedom vs. dictatorship was compounded and often clouded by other factors—the impact of sterilization programs, the dynastic pretentions of Sanjay Gandhi, caste and religious concerns. In the northern areas of India, the heartland of the Hindi language and tradition and a region where religious and minority influences overlap, the governing Congress Party suffered stunning reversals. In the south, it fared exceptionally well. The overall verdict, while being expressed in a most democratic way, was not a total *national* rejection of Mrs. Gandhi's policies and has resulted in a polarized political landscape. The election was a clear demonstration of the effectiveness with which democratic procedures can work (an electorate of approximately 325 million voters, 373 thousand polling stations, and 40 thousand counting centers), but it is still to be proven whether this is a signal of the durability of democracy in India. In the context of recent developments in Pakistan, Bangladesh, and other Asian countries, India appears a major and infrequent exception.

Increasingly, the customary forms of democracy are confined to several North Atlantic nations and a few, mainly industrial, countries outside this region. Among the most vigorous of them, ironically, are two—West Germany and Japan—whose anti-democratic heritage plunged the planet into holocaust and to which democracy was forcibly introduced during the occupation after World War II. As of mid-1977, there were approximately twenty-three democratic states in existence, containing less than 35 percent of the world's population. Even more significant, in those older societies where democratic government was conceived and where it has functioned since its inception, there is that tendency toward serious erosion of democratic practices that we have noted earlier.

The contraction of democracy to the industrialized, free-enterprise countries is subsumed in another vast historical drama. Arnold Toynbee describes it this way:

In these democratically governed—or un-governed—countries, human nature's innate greed is now being given vent shamelessly by citizens of all parties and all classes. The creators of modern mechanized industry have been frankly greedy from the start; they exploited both their own industrial workers and the "native" peoples of the not yet industrialized countries to the utmost of their power, for as long as this power remained in the Western entrepreneurs' hands. In the first act of this unedifying social drama, the victimized Western industrial workers fancied that they were socialists and internationalists; in the current second act, in which, in the Western countries, the balance of power has inclined against the employers in favor of their employees, the industrial workers, now armed with the formidable monopoly-power that they have acquired through the strategy of unionization, have become the most militant advocates of unrestricted economic free enterprise and also of economic, as well as political, nationalism.

Already, however, a third act is being staged. The leaders of "the Third World," which now embraces a decisive and rapidly increasing majority of the living generation of mankind, are copying the strategy of the economically "developed" democratic countries' cartels and trades unions. The balance of power in the World, which, in the West, has already inclined against the employers in favor of their employees, is now beginning to turn against the Western industrial workers themselves in favor of some sections of the poverty-stricken masses of the population of Latin America, Africa, and Asia [*Freedom at Issue*, July-August 1974].

Although Toynbee suggests that the scales are tilting against the industrial democracies, they are still the richest and most powerful segment of the planetary economy. Collectively, they account for almost 65 percent of the world's annual output of wealth and they have a near monopoly on advanced technology and exportable food surpluses. As engines of wealth-creation, they have been primarily responsible for having trebled the economic product of the planet in the period since 1950, thus adding more than twice as much to annual productive power in this past quarter-century as in all the previous existence of humankind. Being in the forefront of this achievement has enabled the industrial economies to accumulate potent assets. However, these industrial democracies now find themselves besieged by a unique combination of internal and external pressures. Three are particularly debilitating, especially to the more capitalist-oriented nations.

The first pressure comes from the inability of capitalist-based industrial society to distribute wealth as competently as it has created it. Therefore, this society has come to be seen by many, inside and outside its confines, as an instrument of inequity. This has resulted in the simultaneous emergence—both within the industrial democracies and between them and their principal sources of energy—of two separate and superimposed demands for a redistribution of wealth. An external demand has led to the quintupling of the price of oil between October 1973 and December 1976. In effect, this represents an annual transfer or oil depletion "tax" of about $100 billion added to the yearly payments made to oil exporters before 1973. The other demand for redistribution is an internal one. It arises from the drive for more equal standards of living and greater monetary rewards created by organized labor. This is most evident in Britain, but there is hardly any major industrial democracy which has not felt its impact recently. "The egalitarian principle, having laid dormant for forty years except for a hiccough in 1945, is on the march again," says *The Economist* newsmagazine. The outcome: Wage increases, which had annually averaged 4 to 7 percent in earlier decades, escalated in the early 1970s to around 10 percent in the United States and as high as 20 to 40 percent in several European nations and Japan.

The convergence of both demands in the early and mid-1970s produced rapid inflation, followed by economic recession in the industrial democracies. These nations could probably cope with each claim by itself, but their economies are unlikely to survive the crushing impact of the simultaneous burden if it is prolonged. Fortunately for them, there is a current abatement in the inflation and wage situation, and desperate attempts to arrange stabilization of oil prices are under way. If more permanent adjustments can be made in either of these two sets of demands, there will be sufficient resilience in the industrial economies for them to stage an effective recovery. If not, the future outlook is clouded and the turmoil of economic strain is likely to have convulsive political and social consequences.

The second pressure on the industrial democracies comes from an internal paradox of capitalism. Diligence, the work ethic, discipline, and organization have been responsible for the success of free-enterprise capitalism. However, as capitalism matures and the consumer economy develops, the goods it produces tend to promote a wasteful and hedonistic society. This, in turn, leads to a weakening of the values necessary to maintain an energetic capitalist environment and promotes listless, unrestrained, or apathetic attitudes. The rugged entrepreneurial spirit dissipates into dependency on government, and the vigor and intellectual imagination that sustains progress is lost. Sociologist Daniel Bell presents a profound analysis of this phenomenon in his study *The Cultural Contradictions of Capitalism*. He writes: "When the Protestant ethic was sundered from bourgeois society, only the hedonism remained and the capitalist system lost its transcendental ethic." To restore the meaning of modern society, Bell calls for a revival of a public philosophy and control of private appetites. This is a hard task requiring continued determination. There are spasmodic signs of this occurring in movements such as environmentalism and consumerism. However, many of the leaders of these efforts are generally unfavorably disposed toward the capitalist system. We have also to see for how long their activities can be sustained and whether these will indeed help preserve capitalism. There is little doubt that the long-term future of capitalist society and its allied political ethos is largely dependent on its capacity to recover its sense of purpose.

The third challenge to the industrial democracies and their economic systems comes from the invalidation of a major supposition that has underwritten their modernization: the idea that the natural resources of the earth would always be available in infinite abundance. The assumed truth of this belief led the pioneers of modernization to consume a vast amount of these resources, while most of the world presumed that there would still be unlimited supplies on which late-comers to the process of economic development could base their own industrialization. However, the ecological and environmental warnings of the past decade, exemplified most strikingly by the oil crisis and the emerging shortages of raw materials, suggest that there clearly are limits to the resources of this planet. If this is so, the price of modern growth by the advanced industrial economies of the world has been paid by the newer nations. By the time these Third World countries are ready to make full use of the earth's natural resources (much of which are located within their own territories), there will be little remaining for them. Their future has been sacrificed for the present affluence of others.

If economic growth can no longer be based on the traditional faith in unlimited resource availability (indeed, continuing such growth may endanger the entire human species), the prospect for the economic self-improvement of the Third World is diminished. To offset this deprivation, Third World nations now ask for compensation from the more prosperous industrial democracies. The United States, with 6 percent of the world's population consuming 35 percent of the world's annual resource output, is an obvious target for these claims. Under some circumstances, such rhetoric can be dismissed as political gimmickry tinged with xenophobic radicalism. But since so much of the earth's remaining unexploited natural resources is located in the Third World, these demands take on a more serious significance, as they could result in vital raw materials being denied to industrial producers.

The charges and demands made by the poorer nations of Asia, the Middle East, Africa, and Latin America also provoke another set of questions: Who, if anyone, is to pay the compensation they seek? How much is to be paid? In what form? Recognition of the importance of the connection between modern industry and its sources of supply gives this matter a fearful urgency. It is at the heart of discussions on a New International Economic Order now being negotiated between the affluent and the poor nations of the world in forums sponsored by the United Nations and other international bodies.

These mounting economic pressures on modern industrial societies bring us back to their relationship to democracy. In times of material abundance, such as much of the post-World War II era, these considerations do not take on a critical importance. However, when scarcity emerges as a continuing and conditioning factor in the world economy, it becomes difficult to satisfy both the demands of the masses and the interests of the dominant classes. Special groups have more of an incentive to capture or use governmental institutions for their own particular purposes. In most Third World countries, the decline in their economic situation has already forced them to abandon democracy and choose between two models of governance: the drastic populism of the type associated with China or the repressive elitism of the sort associated with Brazil. Will the decline in superaffluence in industrial democracies produce similar results and narrow the available political options?

Although these economic issues, with their potentially negative impact on democracy in domestic politics, have moved to the center of the global stage in the 1970s, the decade has also witnessed two developments favorable to democracy evolving on the international scene. There is now an increasingly insistent sentiment for democracy in world affairs. This is often vociferously articulated by nations who have abandoned democratic government at home, but who see its institution in world affairs as their only opportunity to influence a system long dominated by the big powers. Several initiatives in international politics have derived from these demands, notably the United Nations sessions and conferences on a New International Economic Order. Indeed, the United Nations, with all its imperfections and problems, is now a more democratic organization and a more accurate reflection of world opinion than it has ever been. This may not have expanded its effectiveness or power, but it is part of a process which has become unusual in our era: the pursuit of democratization. Perhaps the spirit of democracy at the level of international politics will one day reinfect those nations that have abandoned it domestically and transfer back to their home environment some of the liberties they seek internationally.

A second indirect yet genuine tribute to democracy is seen in developments within the international communist movement. Many major communist parties, especially those in Europe, have been making their own declarations of independence from Soviet control. Not only are they seeking democracy inside their movement, but many claim to espouse democracy in their own national political systems. Perhaps they will some day extend these urges to internal party affairs, which are still conducted on the authoritarian principle of "democratic centralism." In any event, their behavior in recent years is an interesting assertion of democratic rights. These trends, in parts of the world and in organizations scarcely known for their democratic procedures, point to the schizoid possibility of expanding democratic attitudes and impulses at the international level, while such features decline in domestic politics. This may be one of the few ways in which elements of democracy will be preserved for posterity.

PART THREE

THE PROSPECT FOR DEMOCRACY

7   Is There a Future?

Preservation of an intellectual or political system rests primarily on the technical and philosophic resources that it can command. The availability of technology provides the mechanisms through which it can meet the challenges of changing physical conditions and adapt to them. The philosophic strength provides a sense of purpose, enables a commitment to the future, and creates a responsibility to transmit the values of the system to succeeding generations. The lasting and more stable social and spiritual orders of human history have possessed both these attributes; those which have proven transitory have failed to maintain one or the other.

At the present time, democracy has available an impressive range of technical tools. There are three broad categories in which they can be arranged: psychological devices, technological equipment, and organizational developments. Already, a number of these mechanisms are being tested or operated. Since the United States has an early lead in modern technology, much of this discussion will be most immediately relevant to democracy there. However, the implications of these experiments has already begun to reach other nations, especially in the more industrialized portions of the world, and will soon touch more.

Psychological devices and their relationship to today's politics are especially important in two areas. Polling is already an established feature of many political systems; testing is likely to become so. Opinion research is a valuable guide to the issues and the public impacts of policy. It is also a surrogate for democratic elections in providing a reasonably reliable substitute for the ballot by frequently determining the wishes and feelings of the people. By enabling policy making to become more responsive to popular needs, public opinion polls can provide a link between the overburdened leadership of a modern nation and the masses. However, polling can be manipulated to create malevolent results. By combining psychology with technology, unscrupulous politicians can deceive voters. Using polls to find out what people would like to hear and using television to tell it to them, it is possible to mislead citizens into believing that they share a particular viewpoint with a candidate for public office. Additionally, the use of regional polling and local television can produce a situation where the same candidate makes different political appeals in different areas of the country. These dangers can be offset by public-interest monitoring groups and alert national media, but they do suggest possibilities for the abdication of leadership and the enthronement of expedience.

Psychological testing is a method whose time is rapidly drawing near. Given the immense powers of modern government, increasing care will have to be taken to insure that civic positions are held by those who are competent to do so. This is an extension of the physical fitness and financial status disclosures that have become important, although still voluntary, in the electoral processes of several democracies. It is conceivable that forms of psychological screening will, in the future, be applied to those who seek political office and that measures will be devised to eliminate those who are seriously ill-equipped. A delicate balance exists between the individual's right to privacy and the public's right to disclosure, but these procedures contain the potential for improving the quality of political leadership.

In the area of *technology*, television is perhaps the most significant development. There are three ways in which it can, and often does, make a contribution to the workings of democracy. First, in an era of increasingly publicly funded election campaigns, it can have an equalizing influence on candidates for office. Second, it will soon become possible for television to re-create the ancient methods of direct democracy abandoned since the days of Athens; in the not-too-distant future it will be technically feasible for an officeholder to speak to all the citizens in their homes and obtain their reactions. Third, it enables democracy to operate in an entirely new way—through public discussion, agitation, and instruction supplied by the news media. There are several examples in recent U.S. politics (Watergate and its outcome in 1973–74 is one) in which the civic education provided by the mass media played a vital part in urging the elected representatives of the people into effective action. The usefulness of television as a medium of democratic politics relates directly to its sense of public responsibility and the diffusion of its ownership (a state-controlled network, such as that in Italy, France, or India, or a monopoly by one particular interest obviously cannot fulfill this role). Given appropriate precautions and freedom from strong government influence, television can be a major force in democratizing political systems of the future.

There are a number of new *organizational mechanisms* that are evolving in the context of modern democracy. Among these are two innovations in Europe: the efforts at devolution in Britain, and the new structure of the European Parliament. The traditional centralized format of British government has proven inadequate to meet the needs of regional nationalism and development. There is now serious consideration of new forms of regional self-administration for areas such as Scotland. These proposals are controversial and not fully refined, but they offer the promise of revival of intermediate powers between the citizens of a locality with a clearly defined sense of affinity, and the distant state. If this is achieved, devolution could help relieve the overload of modern democracy and restore faith in its capacity to deliver services, while meeting the needs for ethnic or regional identification.

Reform of the European Parliament fits into the pattern of supraregionalism that the European Common Market represents. Conventionally, the Common Market is perceived as a mechanism for coordinating the economies of its nine member-nations. However, it has become a strong influence for democracy both within its boundaries and outside. The new European Parliament, to be chosen by 1978, will enable the citizens of each member country to directly elect representatives to an assembly, which will have authority over certain functions of the Common Market. These elections, to be conducted by democratic processes, will probably have different constituencies and candidates from those for the national legislatures. The Parliament will be a significant step in integrating the political systems of these nine countries into a democratic network and should have a positive effect on the maintenance of democracy within these nations, since the violation of democratic procedures in domestic politics can be checked or protested in a larger forum. The Common Market has, as a group, also become supportive of democratic forces on its borders. Pressures on the governments of Portugal, Greece, and Spain and assistance to democratic parties within each have been of vital importance in moving these nations away from authoritarianism since 1974.

The growth of industrial democracy is another recent European innovation. Under this system workers are given the right of participation in policy decisions of business corporations. The aim of this effort is to democratize the authoritarian structure of powerful institutions in the private sector of the economy and so to infuse managerial capitalism with elements of democracy. In 1976, Sweden and West Germany enacted laws to implement these concepts; several other European nations will soon follow. The progressive adoption of this principle in various segments of the economy will strengthen the idea of participation and representation in economic affairs.

In addition to industrial democracy, several other organizational changes are taking place in the political life of democratic nations. These include the extension of voting rights to those between the ages of eighteen and twenty-one and the development of new methods of mobilization, which can be applied to large groups of people.

This array of technological strengths and techniques equips modern democracy to meet many of the physical demands of a fast changing environment. However, all the tools of technology are of minor consequence, if there is no philosophic dedication to make them work. Modern democracy here encounters a challenge that will ultimately decide its fate, and it is here where it is beginning to show serious weaknesses. Not only is the general commitment to democratic values diminishing, but democracy now has a crisis of definition—an uncertainty concerning the conception of the human character. Is it to be formed in the personality of a freedom-seeking person, and, if so, what are the limits of self-discipline on freedom? Is human talent to be put at the service of the state, and productivity and discipline placed above liberty? Is retreat into romantic commune life and harmony with nature, abandoning social institutions along the way, the answer? To what purpose does democracy shape the human being?

Earlier societies had clear notions of the exemplary character, and this helped to create a meaning and an aspiration for individuals in relation to their political order. For several centuries, religion outlined this vision. In the nineteenth and early twentieth centuries, science took over, and the promise of modern civilization, originally idealistic, became materialist. But we are now aware of the limits and the moral neutrality of science; being neither good nor bad in itself, it has little to say about the purpose of the human character in the political context. In Marxist nations, this vacuum does not exist; the exemplary character can be either real or imaginary, but it dominates Soviet and Marxist thought. Democracy in our time has still to produce a counterpart character who will have a purpose beyond survival as a goal. This is the philosophic agony of modern democracy, the testing ground of its future and of its destiny.

Will democracy disappear or does it have the capacity for self-renewal? Because there are so many different situations and different forces at work, the question must be asked of three different contexts: the industrialized democracies, the Third World, and the Marxist countries.

The first group of nations are those in which democracy already exists as a viable political system. Few in number, they have several common characteristics: relative affluence; a high degree of industrialization; high rates of literacy; and an expanding and property-owning middle class. Although we have noted a general decline in the mechanisms of democracy, these states have maintained many of its essentials, and democracy is unlikely to come to any sudden end in them, at least among the most significant. The threat to democracy there is more in its gradual erosion over a long period of time. While there appears to be connection between wide-spread literacy, affluence, property ownership, and the stability of democracy, there is also the possibility that a weakening of any one of these elements may create an atmosphere of the type which caused a sophisticated nation, such as Germany, to abandon democracy in the early 1930s. At present, those signals show faintly in Britain and Italy, but unless developments of a catastrophic nature occur, democracy appears durable in this segment of the political world.

An important question for these nations is not whether democracy will vanish, but whether they have the capacity to revive its more vigorous forms. The uses of technology and several other signs indicate that this is possible, but there is no hard evidence that it has yet become a reality. Gradual debilitation can take a considerable while to afflict the body politic, but dramatic recoveries can also happen along the way.

Does the high level of literacy and affluence in many democracies indicate that as newer nations become more prosperous and better formally educated, they will become more democratic? The chances of this occurring appear very limited, especially in the absence of deep-seated democratic traditions. Several Marxist-oriented countries have improved their living standards and rapidly increased their educational resources. Despite occasional activities to the contrary, they do not appear ready in the foreseeable future to adopt democracy as their system of government. The authoritarian states with free-enterprise economies are as unlikely to do this. Taiwan and Brazil are among those with the best economic performances, but they show little inclination to turn into democracies. Japan and Germany provide interesting exceptions. Historically, both have had advanced rates of literacy, but no extensive experience with democratic politics. Yet a democratic system imposed after World War II has taken root and seems reasonably secure. It can be argued, then, that there is insufficient evidence to underwrite the proposition that upward progress in literacy and living standards will result in the natural evolution of democracy. It can, however, also be claimed that these are effective supports to democracy when it is established.

A second area of analysis provides a clearer conclusion: Poverty, slow economic growth, and conditions of social deprivation tend to work against democracy. This is the lesson of the Third World, where democracy has been largely rejected for authoritarian forms of government. The urgencies of the Third World concern development and the building of a new social order. To satisfy these priorities, they are prepared to sacrifice democratic rights—individuals cannot survive on liberties alone. Even India, which proudly sustained a vibrant democratic environment for twenty-five years, did succumb to a combination of economic and political pressures in 1975. A surface assessment would conclude that the democratic prospect is meager in the Third World. However, an interesting situation could arise at some future time. If authoritarian systems are unable to make significant economic and social gains, as many may be unable to do, will democracy emerge as an alternative? Or will these nations edge further toward a totalitarian abyss? Several instances, of which China is the most compelling, suggest that the latter will occur. But it may be premature to make so definitive a judgment.

A third group of nations are those governed, to a greater or lesser degree, by the tenets of Marxism. The acceptance of democracy as a replacement for their present system seems remote. Within the circumstances of communism, there have been indications that some democratic elements can occasionally seep into these societies. Witness the activity of dissidents in the Soviet Union, protest demonstrations in Poland, sporadic opportunities for open expression in Yugoslavia, and discussions about enabling non-party candidates to compete against Communist Party nominees in Cuba. These are, of course, not genuine democratizations as they are traditionally conceived, but rather liberalizing concessions granted or tolerated by the regime. Real democratic impulses in both the Third and Marxist Worlds seem to be currently expressed more in the international arena than in domestic politics.

In summary, this survey does not offer any serious and near hope for a major expansion of democracy outside those areas where it presently functions. At best, we can expect some democratic tendencies to prevail, but not to develop into any major movements. In those nations where democracy has been preserved we can expect it to continue, but there are symptoms of an atrophy of its mechanisms, a weakening of the philosophic commitment, and the danger of a collapse precipitated by economic emergencies. In these countries, there is also the potential for revitalization and renewal. Observing this prospect, we must reluctantly conclude that it is not an encouraging vision and contains little evidence that democracy will be the wave of the remaining decades of the twentieth century.

Epilogue

As I read and reread these writings, I feel a profound sense of drama, if not tragedy. Democracy is an ideal that has inspired the noblest sentiments of human civilization. Many men and women have died in its cause. Tyranny and oppression have been fought and defeated in its name. Its charisma has extended even to its opponents, who cloak themselves in its form while they attack its substance. For most of the past century, it has promised a better and more humane world. Yet today democracy is an embattled political system in the midst of a crisis of faith and of practice. The modern democratic experience appears as a brief interlude, a short flowering of freedom, in the human record of political injustice and oppression. Have, then, the labors and the dedication of so many ultimately been in vain, their values and hopes misplaced? There is no easy answer to this question, for each of us must address it from the depths of our own philosophic beliefs.

As we do so, we must remember that the expectations for democracy have far exceeded its capacity; the reality has never been able to match the ideal. It is also clear that the traditional concept of democracy, the product of two centuries of effort, is passing into history. Like the ancient Greeks, in their time, we are witnesses to this decline. And yet, democracy has had a dramatic impact on the modern world, in shaping both great political events and other ideologies. Its customs and forms may evaporate, but its heritage will live on in adaptations and mutations that will also be called "democracy." The needs and the characters of societies tend to define their

105

ideologies. Democracy arose in a time when the values of liberty and self-determination outranked all others. New urgencies have created new priorities and political environments have responded accordingly. If we seek to restore democracy, we must first renew the values that gave it birth.

CHARTER DOCUMENTS
OF DEMOCRACY

The U.S. Declaration of Independence, 1776

IN CONGRESS, JULY 4, 1776

A DECLARATION

BY THE REPRESENTATIVES OF THE

UNITED STATES OF AMERICA,

IN GENERAL CONGRESS ASSEMBLED.

WHEN in the Course of human Events, it becomes necessary for one People to dissolve the Political Bands which have connected them with another, and to assume among the Powers of the Earth, the separate and equal Station to which the Laws of Nature and of Nature's God entitle them, a decent Respect to the Opinions of Mankind requires that they should declare the causes which impel them to the Separation.

WE hold these Truths to be self-evident, that all Men are created equal, that they are endowed by their Creator with certain unalienable Rights, that among these are Life, Liberty and the Pursuit of Happiness —That to secure these Rights, Governments are instituted among Men, deriving their just Power from the Consent of the Governed, that whenever any Form of Government becomes destructive of these Ends, it is the Right of the People to alter or to abolish it, and to institute new Government, laying its Foundation on such Principles, and organizing its Powers in such Form, as to them shall seem most likely to effect their Safety and Happiness. Prudence, indeed, will dictate that Governments long established should not be changed for light and transient Causes; and accordingly all Experience hath shewn, that Mankind are more disposed to suffer, while Evils are sufferable, than to right themselves by abolishing the Forms to which they are accustomed. But when a long Train of Abuses and Usurpations, pursuing invariably the same Object, evinces a Design to reduce them under absolute Despotism, it is their Right, it is their Duty, to throw off such Government, and to provide new Guards for their future Security. Such has been the patient Sufferance of these Colonies; and such is now the Necessity which constrains them to alter their former Systems of Government. The History of the present King of Great Britain is a History of repeated Injuries and Usurpations, all having in direct Object the Establishment of an absolute Tyranny over these States. To prove this, let Facts be submitted to a candid World.

HE has refused his Assent to Laws, the most wholesome and necessary for the public Good.

HE has forbidden his Governors to pass Laws of immediate and pressing Importance, unless suspended in their Operation till his Assent should be obtained; and when so suspended, he has utterly neglected to attend to them.

HE has refused to pass other Laws for the Accommodation of large Districts of People, unless those People would relinquish the Right of Representation in the Legislature, a Right inestimable to them and formidable to Tyrants only.

HE has called together Legislative Bodies at Places unusual, uncomfortable, and distant from the Depository of their public Records, for the sole Purpose of fatiguing them into Compliance with his Measures.

HE has dissolved Representative Houses repeatedly, for opposing with manly Firmness his invasions on the Rights of the People.

HE has refused for a long Time, after such Dissolutions, to cause others to be elected; whereby the Legislative Powers, incapable of Annihilation, have returned to the People at large for their exercise; the State remaining in the meantime exposed to all the Dangers of Invasion from without, and Convulsions within.

HE has endeavoured to prevent the Population of these States; for that Purpose obstructing the Laws for Naturalization of Foreigners; refusing to pass others to encourage their Migrations hither, and raising the Conditions of new Appropriations of Lands.

HE has obstructed the Administration of Justice, by refusing his Assent to Laws for establishing Judiciary Powers.

HE has made Judges dependent on his Will alone, for the Tenure of their Offices, and the Amount and Payment of their Salaries.

HE has erected a Multitude of new Offices, and sent hither Swarms of Officers to harass our People, and eat out their Substance.

HE has kept among us, in Times of Peace, Standing Armies, without the consent of our Legislatures.

HE has affected to render the Military independent of and superior to the Civil Power.

HE has combined with others to subject us to a Jurisdiction foreign to our Constitution, and unacknowledged by our Laws; giving his Assent to their Acts of pretended Legislation:

FOR quartering large Bodies of Armed Troops among us:

FOR protecting them, by a mock Trial, from Punishment for any Murders which they should commit on the Inhabitants of these States:

FOR cutting off our Trade with all Parts of the World:

FOR imposing Taxes on us without our Consent:

FOR depriving us, in many Cases, of the Benefits of Trial by Jury:

FOR transporting us beyond Seas to be tried for pretended Offences:

FOR abolishing the free System of English Laws in a neighbouring Province, establishing therein an arbitrary Government, and enlarging its Boundaries, so as to render it at once an Example and fit Instrument of introducing the same absolute Rule into these Colonies:

FOR taking away our Charters, abolishing our most valuable Laws, and altering fundamentally the Forms of our Governments:

FOR suspending our own Legislatures, and declaring themselves invested with Power to legislate for us in all Cases whatsoever.

HE has abdicated Government here, by declaring us out of his Protection and waging War against us.

HE has plundered our Seas, ravaged our Coasts, burnt our Towns, and destroyed the Lives of our People.

HE is, at this Time, transporting large Armies of foreign Mercenaries to compleat the Works of Death, Desolation, and Tyranny, already begun with circumstances of Cruelty and Perfidy, scarcely paralleled in the most barbarous Ages, and totally unworthy of the Head of a civilized Nation.

HE has constrained our fellow Citizens taken Captive on the high Seas to bear Arms against their Country, to become the Executioners of their Friends and Brethren, or to fall themselves by their Hands.

HE has excited domestic Insurrections amongst us, and has endeavoured to bring on the Inhabitants of our Frontiers, the merciless Indian Savages, whose known Rule of Warfare, is an undistinguished Destruction of all Ages, Sexes and Conditions.

IN every stage of these Oppressions we have Petitioned for Redress in the most humble Terms: Our repeated Petitions have been answered only by repeated Injury. A Prince, whose Character is thus marked by every act which may define a Tyrant, is unfit to be the Ruler of a free People.

NOR have we been wanting in Attentions to our British Brethren. We have warned them from Time to

Time of Attempts by their Legislature to extend an unwarrantable Jurisdiction over us. We have reminded them of the Circumstances of our Emigration and Settlement here. We have appealed to their native Justice and Magnanimity, and we have conjured them by the Ties of our common Kindred to disavow these Usurpations, which, would inevitably interrupt our Connections and Correspondence. They too have been deaf to the Voice of Justice and of Consanguinity. We must, therefore, acquiesce in the Necessity, which denounces our Separation, and hold them, as we hold the rest of Mankind, Enemies in War, in Peace, Friends.

We, therefore, the representatives of the UNITED STATES OF AMERICA, in GENERAL CONGRESS, Assembled, appealing to the Supreme Judge of the World for the Rectitude of our Intentions, do, in the Name, and by Authority of the good People of these Colonies, solemnly Publish and Declare, That these United Colonies are, and of Right ought to be, FREE AND INDEPENDENT STATES; that they are absolved from all Allegiance to the British Crown, and that all political Connection between them and the State of Great Britain, is and ought to be totally dissolved; and that as FREE AND INDEPENDENT STATES, they have full Power to levy War, conclude Peace, contract Alliances, establish Commerce, and to do all other Acts and Things which INDEPENDENT STATES may of right do. And for the support of this Declaration, with a firm Reliance on the Protection of divine Providence, we mutually pledge to each other our Lives, our Fortunes, and our sacred Honor.

Signed by ORDER *and in*
BEHALF *of the* CONGRESS,
JOHN HANCOCK, PRESIDENT

ATTEST.
CHARLES THOMSON, SECRETARY.

The French Declaration of the Rights of Man and of the Citizen, 1789

Decreed by the National Assembly of France in sessions of 20, 21, 22, 23, 24, and 26 August 1789

Signed by the King on 5 October 1789

PREAMBLE

The representatives of the French people, organized in the National Assembly, considering that ignorance, forgetfulness or contempt of the rights of man are the sole causes of the public miseries and of the corruption of governments, have resolved to set forth in a solemn declaration the natural, inalienable, and sacred rights of man, in order that this declaration, being ever present to all the members of the social body, may unceasingly remind them of their rights and duties; in order that the acts of the legislative power and those of the executive power may be each moment compared with the aim of every political institution and thereby may be more respected; and in order that the demands of the citizens, grounded henceforth upon simple and incontestable principles, may always take the direction of maintaining the constitution and the welfare of all. In consequence, the National Assembly recognizes and declares in the presence and under the auspices of the

Supreme Being, the following rights of man and of the citizen:

ARTICLE I

Men are born and remain free and equal in rights. Social distinctions can be based only upon public utility.

II

The aim of every political association is the preservation of the natural and imprescriptible rights of man. These rights are liberty, property, security and resistance to oppression.

III

The source of all sovereignty is essentially in the nation; no body, no individual can exercise authority that does not proceed from it in plain terms.

IV

Liberty consists in the power to do anything that does not injure others; accordingly, the exercise of the natural rights of each man has for its only limits those that secure to the other members of society the enjoyment of these same rights. These limits can be determined only by law.

V

The law has the right to forbid only such actions as are injurious to society. Nothing can be forbidden that is not interdicted by the law, and no one can be constrained to do that which it does not order.

VI

Law is the expression of the general will. All citizens have the right to take part personally or by their representatives in its formation. It must be the same for all, whether it protects or punishes. All citizens being equal in its eyes, are equally eligible to all public dignities, places, employments, according to their capacities, and without other distinction than that of their virtues and their talents.

VII

No man can be accused, arrested or detained except in the cases determined by the law and according to the forms that it has prescribed. Those who procure, expedite, execute or cause to be executed arbitrary orders ought to be punished; but every citizen summoned or seized in virtue of the law ought to render instant obedience; he makes himself guilty by resistance.

VIII

The law ought to establish only penalties that are strictly and obviously necessary and no one can be punished except in virtue of a law established and promulgated prior to the offence and legally applied.

IX

Every man being presumed innocent until he has been pronounced guilty, if it is thought indispensable to arrest him, all severity that may not be necessary to secure his person ought to be strictly suppressed by law.

X

No one ought to be disturbed on account of his opinions, even religious, provided their manifestation does not derange the public order established by law.

XI

The free communication of ideas and opinions is one of the most precious of the rights of man; every citizen can freely speak, write, and print, subject to responsibility for the abuse of this freedom in the cases determined by law.

XII

The guarantee of the rights of man and of the citizen requires a public force; this force then is instituted for the advantage of all and not for the personal benefit of those to whom it is entrusted.

XIII

For the maintenance of the public force and for the expenses of administration a general tax is indispensable; it ought to be equally apportioned among all the citizens according to their means.

XIV

All the citizens have the right to ascertain, by themselves or by their representatives, the necessity of the public tax, to consent to it freely, to follow the employment of it, and to determine the quota, the assessment, the collection and the duration of it.

XV

Society has the right to call for an account from every public agent of its administration.

XVI

Any society in which the guarantee of the rights is not secured or the separation of powers not determined has no constitution at all.

XVII

Property being a sacred and inviolable right, no one can be deprived of it unless a legal established public necessity evidently demands it, under the condition of a just and prior indemnity.

The British Bill of Rights, 1689

[The Bill of Rights* was a document condemning the conduct of King James II and setting forth the condition upon which the British throne was offered to William and Mary of Holland in 1688. After their acceptance and accession to the monarchy, the Bill of Rights became an Act of the British Parliament in 1689. It included the following principal articles.]

That the pretended power of suspending laws, or of execution of laws, by regal authority without consent of parliament, is illegal.

That the pretended power of dispensing with laws, or the execution of laws, by regal authority, as it hath been assumed and exercised of late, is illegal.

That it is the right of the subjects to petition the king, and all commitments and prosecutions for such petitioning are illegal.

That the freedom of speech, and debates or proceedings in parliament, ought not to be impeached or questioned in any court or place out of parliament.

That excessive bail ought not to be required, nor excessive fines imposed, nor cruel and unusual punishments inflicted.

That all grants and promises of fines and forfeitures of particular persons before convictions are illegal and void.

---

*The British Bill of Rights should not be confused with the American Bill of Rights. The latter refers to the first ten amendments of the Constitution of the United States, which were ratified in December 1791, four years after the Constitutional Convention.

The U.N. Universal Declaration of Human Rights, 1948

[On December 10, 1948, the General Assembly of the United Nations adopted and proclaimed the Universal Declaration of Human Rights.]

PREAMBLE

Whereas recognition of the inherent dignity and of the equal and inalienable rights of all members of the human family is the foundation of freedom, justice and peace in the world,

Whereas disregard and contempt for human rights have resulted in barbarous acts which have outraged the conscience of mankind, and the advent of a world in which human beings shall enjoy freedom of speech and belief and freedom from fear and want has been proclaimed as the highest aspiration of the common people,

Whereas it is essential, if man is not to be compelled to have recourse, as a last resort, to rebellion against tyranny and oppression, that human rights should be protected by the rule of law,

Whereas it is essential to promote the development of friendly relations between nations,

Whereas the peoples of the United Nations have in the Charter reaffirmed their faith in fundamental human rights, in the dignity and worth of the human person and in the equal rights of men and women and have

119

determined to promote social progress and better standards of life in larger freedom,

Whereas Member States have pledged themselves to achieve in co-operation with the United Nations, the promotion of universal respect for and observance of human rights and fundamental freedoms,

Whereas a common understanding of these rights and freedoms is of the greatest importance for the full realization of this pledge,

Now, Therefore,

THE GENERAL ASSEMBLY

proclaims

THIS UNIVERSAL DECLARATION OF HUMAN RIGHTS as a common standard of achievement for all peoples and all nations, to the end that every individual and every organ of society, keeping this Declaration constantly in mind, shall strive by teaching and education to promote respect for these rights and freedoms and by progressive measures, national and international, to secure their universal and effective recognition and observance, both among the peoples of Member States themselves and among the peoples of territories under their jurisdiction.

Article 1. All human beings are born free and equal in dignity and rights. They are endowed with reason and conscience and should act towards one another in a spirit of brotherhood.

Article 2. Everyone is entitled to all the rights and freedoms set forth in this Declaration, without distinction of any kind, such as race, colour, sex, language, religion, political or other opinion, national or social origin, property, birth or other status.

Furthermore, no distinction shall be made on the basis of the political, jurisdictional or international status of the country or territory to which a person belongs, whether it be independent, trust, non-self-governing or under any other limitation of sovereignty.

Article 3. Everyone has the right to life, liberty and security of person.

Article 4. No one shall be held in slavery or servitude; slavery and the slave trade shall be prohibited in all their forms.

Article 5. No one shall be subjected to torture or to cruel, inhuman or degrading treatment or punishment.

Article 6. Everyone has the right to recognition everywhere as a person before the law.

Article 7. All are equal before the law and are entitled without any discrimination to equal protection of the law. All are entitled to equal protection against any discrimination in violation of this Declaration and against any incitement to such discrimination.

Article 8. Everyone has the right to an effective remedy by the competent national tribunals for acts violating the fundamental rights granted him by the constitution or by law.

Article 9. No one shall be subjected to arbitrary arrest, detention or exile.

Article 10. Everyone is entitled in full equality to a fair and public hearing by an independent and impartial tribunal, in the determination of his rights and obligations and of any criminal charge against him.

Article 11. (1) Everyone charged with a penal offence has the right to be presumed innocent until proved guilty according to law in a public trial at which he has had all the guarantees necessary for his defence.

(2) No one shall be held guilty of any penal offence on account of any act or omission which did not constitute a penal offence, under national or international law, at the time when it was committed. Nor shall a heavier penalty be imposed than the one that was applicable at the time the penal offence was committed.

Article 12. No one shall be subjected to arbitrary interference with his privacy, family, home or correspondence, nor to attacks upon his honour and reputation. Everyone has the right to the protection of the law against such interference or attacks.

Article 13. (1) Everyone has the right to freedom of movement and residence within the borders of each state.

(2) Everyone has the right to leave any country, including his own, and to return to his country.

Article 14. (1) Everyone has the right to seek and to enjoy in other countries asylum from persecution.

(2) This right may not be invoked in the case of prosecutions genuinely arising from non-political crimes or from acts contrary to the purposes and principles of the United Nations.

Article 15. (1) Everyone has the right to a nationality.

(2) No one shall be arbitrarily deprived of his nationality nor denied the right to change his nationality.

Article 16. (1) Men and women of full age, without any limitation due to race, nationality or religion, have the right to marry and to found a family. They are entitled to equal rights as to marriage, during marriage and at its dissolution.

(2) Marriage shall be entered into only with the free and full consent of the intending spouses.

(3) The family is the natural and fundamental group unit of society and is entitled to protection by society and the State.

Article 17. (1) Everyone has the right to own property alone as well as in association with others.

(2) No one shall be arbitrarily deprived of his property.

Article 18. Everyone has the right to freedom of thought, conscience and religion; this right includes freedom to change his religion or belief, and freedom, either alone or in community with others and in public or private, to manifest his religion or belief in teaching, practice, worship and observance.

Article 19. Everyone has the right to freedom of opinion and expression; this right includes freedom to hold opinions without interference and to seek, receive and impart information and ideas through any media and regardless of frontiers.

Article 20. (1) Everyone has the right to freedom of peaceful assembly and association.

(2) No one may be compelled to belong to an association.

Article 21. (1) Everyone has the right to take part in the government of his country, directly or through freely chosen representatives.

(2) Everyone has the right of equal access to public service in his country.

(3) The will of the people shall be the basis of the authority of government; this will shall be expressed in periodic and genuine elections which shall be by universal and equal suffrage and shall be held by secret vote or by equivalent free voting procedures.

Article 22. Everyone, as a member of society, has the right to social security and is entitled to realization, through national effort and international co-operation and in accordance with the organization and resources of each State, of the economic, social and cultural rights indispensable for his dignity and the free development of his personality.

Article 23. (1) Everyone has the right to work, to free choice of employment, to just and favourable conditions of work and to protection against unemployment.

(2) Everyone, without any discrimination, has the right to equal pay for equal work.

(3) Everyone who works has the right to just and favourable remuneration ensuring for himself and his family an existence worthy of human dignity, and supplemented, if necessary, by other means of social protection.

(4) Everyone has the right to form and to join trad unions for the protection of his interests.

Article 24. Everyone has the right to rest and leisure, including reasonable limitation of working hours and periodic holidays with pay.

Article 25. (1) Everyone has the right to a standard of living adequate for the health and well-being of himself and of his family, including food, clothing, housing and medical care and necessary social services, and the right to security in the event of unemployment, sickness, disability, widowhood, old age or other lack of livelihood in circumstances beyond his control.

(2) Motherhood and childhood are entitled to special care and assistance. All children, whether born in or out of wedlock, shall enjoy the same social protection.

Article 26. (1) Everyone has the right to education. Education shall be free, at least in the elementary and fundamental stages. Elementary education shall be compulsory. Technical and professional education shall be made generally available and higher education shall be equally accessible to all on the basis of merit.

(2) Education shall be directed to the full development of the human personality and to the strengthening of respect for human rights and fundamental freedoms. It shall promote understanding, tolerance and friendship among all nations, racial or religious groups, and shall further the activities of the United Nations for the maintenance of peace.

(3) Parents have a prior right to choose the kind of education that shall be given to their children.

Article 27. (1) Everyone has the right freely to participate in the cultural life of the community, to enjoy the arts and to share in scientific advancement and its benefits.

(2) Everyone has the right to the protection of the moral and material interests resulting from any scientific, literary or artistic production of which he is the author.

Article 28. Everyone is entitled to a social and international order in which the rights and freedoms set forth in this Declaration can be fully realized.

Article 29. (1) Everyone has duties to the community in which alone the free and full development of his personality is possible.

(2) In the exercise of his rights and freedoms, everyone shall be subject only to such limitations as are determined by law solely for the purpose of securing due recognition and respect for the rights and freedoms of others and of meeting the just requirements of morality, public order and the general welfare in a democratic society.

(3) These rights and freedoms may in no case be exercised contrary to the purposes and principles of the United Nations.

Article 30. Nothing in this Declaration may be interpreted as implying for any State, group or person any right to engage in any activity or to perform any act aimed at the destruction of any of the rights and freedoms set forth herein.

SELECTED QUOTATIONS ON DEMOCRACY

The seventy quotations in this appendix represent a random sampling of the many observations made about democracy. Except for the first group, they are all derived from writings or statements made in the past two centuries. This is not, in any way, a comprehensive compilation but reflects a subjective selection of many profound, amusing, and sometimes depressing remarks on democracy.

The Ancients
Reject Democracy

ARISTOTLE

Democracy arose from men thinking that if they are equal in any respect they are equal in all respects [*Politics*, V, c. 332 B.C.].

A democracy is a government in the hands of men of low birth, no property, and vulgar employments [*Politics*, VI, c. 332 B.C.].

PLATO

A democracy is a state in which the poor, gaining the upper hand, kill some and banish others, and then divide the offices among the remaining citizens equally, usually by lot [*The Republic*, VIII, c. 370 B.C.].

Democracy is a charming form of government, full of variety and disorder, dispensing a kind of equality to equals and unequals alike [*The Republic*, VIII, c. 370 B.C.].

The excessive increase of anything causes a reaction in the opposite direction; ... dictatorship naturally arises out of democracy, and the most aggravated form of tyranny and slavery out of the most extreme form of liberty [*The Republic*, V, c. 370 B.C.].

POLYBIUS

When a state increases in wealth and luxury men indulge in ambitious projects and are eager for high dignities. Each feels ashamed that any of his fellow men should surpass him. The common people feel themselves oppressed by the grasping of some, and their vanity is flattered by others. Fired with evil passions, they are no longer willing to submit to control, but demand that everything be subject to their authority. The invariable result is that the government assumes the noble names of free and popular, but becomes in fact that most execrable thing, mob rule [*Histories*, VI, c. 125 B.C.].

SENECA

Democracy is more cruel than war or tyrants [*Epistulae Morales Ad Lucilium*, CIV, c. 53 A.D.].

The Foundations of
Modern Democracy

SIMON BOLIVAR

Only democracy, in my opinion, is capable of providing absolute freedom. But where is the democratic government that has managed to combine at a given moment power, prosperity, and permanency? ... Codes of laws, systems, constitutions, however wisely drawn up, are dead letters which have little effect upon human societies. It is honest men, patriots, illustrious human beings—it is these who make up a Republic [Speech to the Assembly of Angostura, Venezuela, February 15, 1819].

EDWARD HALLETT CARR

Modern democracy, as it grew up and spread from its focus in western Europe, over the past three centuries, rested on three main propositions: first, that the individual conscience is the ultimate source of decisions about what is right and wrong; second, that there exists between different individuals a fundamental harmony of interests strong enough to enable them to live peacefully together in society; third, that where action has to be taken in the name of society, rational discussion between individuals is the best method of reaching a decision on that action. Modern democracy is, in virtue of its origins, individualist, optimistic and rational. The three main propositions on which it is based have all been seriously challenged in the contemporary world [*The New Society*, 1957].

131

MOHANDAS (MAHATMA) GANDHI

My notion of democracy is that under it the weakest should have the same opportunity as the strongest. That can never happen except through nonviolence [Interview, April 1940].

THOMAS JEFFERSON

The will of the people is the only legitimate foundation of any government [Letter to B. Waring, 1801].

The freedom and happiness of man ... are the sole objectives of all legitimate governments [Letter to Tadeusz Kosciuszko, 1810].

I have no fear, but that the result of our experiment will be, that men may be trusted to govern themselves without a master. Could the contrary of this be proved, I should conclude, either that there is no God, or that he is a malevolent being [Letter to David Hartley, 1787].

JAMES MADISON

In framing a government which is to be administered by men over men, the great difficulty lies in this: You must enable the government to control the governed; and in the place oblige it to control itself [*The Federalist*, no. 51, 1788].

HANS MORGENTHAU

Democratic government is government by popular choice—choice of men and, through it, choice of policy. A government that can keep itself in power regardless of the preferences of the people is not democratic at all; a government whose choice by the people does not also imply a choice of policy is but imperfectly so. It follows that a perfectly democratic system of government must be partisan government in the sense that those who have been elected to govern stand for one set of policies and those who have been rejected at the polls are committed to another set of policies. The candidates for office have been judged by the policies with which they are identified and by their ability to carry them through, and at the next elections they will again be judged by these criteria [*The New Republic*, December 17, 1956].

JAWAHARLAL NEHRU

Democracy did not, of course, say that all men were in fact equal. It could not say this, because it is obvious enough that there are inequalities between different men.... So far as democracy is concerned, it admitted that men were as a matter of fact unequal, and yet it stated that each one of them should be treated as having an equal political and social value [*Glimpses of World History*, 1934].

FRANKLIN D. ROOSEVELT

There is nothing mysterious about the foundations of a healthy and strong democracy. The basic things expected by our people of their political and economic systems are simple. They are: equality of opportunity for youth and for others; jobs for those who can work; security for those who need it; the ending of special privilege for the few; the preservation of civil liberties for all; the enjoyment of the fruits of scientific progress in a wider and constantly rising standard of living.

These are the simple and basic things that must never be lost sight of in the turmoil and unbelievable complexity of our modern world. The inner and abiding strength of our economic and political systems is dependent upon the degree to which they fulfill these expectations.

In future days, which we seek to make secure, we look

forward to a world founded upon four essential human freedoms.

The first is freedom of speech and expression—everywhere in the world.

The second is freedom of every person to worship God in his own way—everywhere in the world.

The third is freedom from want—which, translated into world terms, means economic understandings which will secure to every nation a healthy peace-time life for its inhabitants—everywhere in the world.

The fourth is freedom from fear—which, translated into world terms, means world-wide reduction of armaments to such a point and in such a thorough fashion that no nation will be in a position to commit an act of physical aggression against any neighbor—anywhere in the world.

That is no vision of a distant millenium. It is a definite basis for a kind of world attainable in our own time and generation. That kind of world is the very antithesis of the so-called new order of tyranny which the dictators seek to create with the crash of a bomb.

To that new order we oppose the greater conception—the moral order. A good society is able to face schemes of world domination and foreign revolutions alike without fear ["Four Freedoms" Speech, January 6, 1941].

JOHANN FRIEDRICH VON SCHILLER

Political and civil liberty is and will always be the most sacred of all blessings, the worthiest object of all endeavor, and the nucleus of all culture: but the only firm foundation on which this glorious edifice can ever be erected is nobility of mind. We have to begin, therefore, by creating the citizens for a Constitution, before we can give a Constitution to the citizens [*History of the Thirty Years War*, 1790].

ALFRED E. SMITH

All the ills of democracy can be cured by more democracy [Speech in Albany, June 27, 1933].

GEORGE WASHINGTON

The basis of our political systems is the right of the people to make and to alter their constitutions of government. But the constitution which at any time exists till changed by an explicit and authentic act of the whole people is sacredly obligatory upon all. The very idea of the power and the right of the people to establish government presupposes the duty of every individual to obey the established government [Farewell Address, 1796].

DANIEL WEBSTER

The people's government made for the people, made by the people, and answerable to the people [Speech to the United States Senate, 1830].

The Democratic Environment

JOHN EMERICH, LORD ACTON

The fate of every democracy, of every government based on the sovereignty of the people, depends on the choice it makes between these opposite principles: absolute power on the one hand, and on the other the restraints of legality and the authority of tradition. It must stand or fall according to its choice, whether to give the supremacy to the law or to the will of the people; whether to constitute a moral association maintained by duty, or a physical one kept together by force [*Political Causes of the American Revolution*, 1861].

ALEXIS DE TOCQUEVILLE

The public has therefore among a democratic people a singular power, of which aristocratic nations could never so much as conceive an idea; for it does not persuade them to certain opinions, but enforces them, and infuses into them the faculties by a sort of enormous pressure of the minds of all upon the reason of each [*Democracy in America*, 1835].

WILL AND ARIEL DURANT

Most governments have been oligarchies—ruled by a minority, chosen either by birth, as in aristocracies, or by a religious organization, as in theocracies, or by wealth, as in democracies. It is unnatural (as even Rousseau saw) for a majority to rule, for a majority can seldom be organized for united and specific action, and a minority can. If the majority of abilities is contained in a

136

minority of men, minority government is as inevitable as the concentration of wealth; the majority can do no more than periodically throw out one minority and set up another [*The Lessons of History*, 1968].

MOHANDAS (MAHATMA) GANDHI

A born democrat is a born disciplinarian. Democracy comes naturally to him who is habituated normally to yield willing obedience to all laws, human or divine. I claim to be a democrat both by instinct and training. Let those who are ambitious to serve democracy qualify themselves by satisfying first this acid test of democracy. Moreover, a democrat must be utterly selfless. He must think and dream not in terms of self or party but only of democracy. Only then does he acquire the right of civil disobedience. I do not want anybody to give up his convictions or to suppress himself. I do not believe that a healthy and honest difference of opinion will injure our cause. But opportunism, camouflage or patched up compromises certainly will. If you must dissent, you should take care that your opinions voice your innermost convictions and are not intended merely as a convenient party cry [*Harijan*, May 27, 1939].

Democracy disciplined and enlightened is the finest thing in the world. A democracy prejudiced, ignorant, superstitious will land itself in chaos and may be self-destroyed [*Young India*, July 30, 1931].

Democracy and violence can ill go together. The States that are today nominally democratic have either to become frankly totalitarian or if they are to become truly democratic, they must become courageously nonviolent. It is a blasphemy to say that nonviolence can be practiced by individuals and never by nations which are composed of individuals [*Harijan*, November 12, 1938].

THOMAS JEFFERSON

Every man, and every body of men on earth, possess the right of self-government. They receive it with their being from the hand of nature. Individuals exercise it by their single will; collections of men by that of their majority; for the law of the *majority* is the natural law of every society of men [Statement on the transfer of the seat of Government to the Potomac, 1790].

There is a natural aristocracy among men. The grounds of this are virtue and talents. . . . The natural aristocracy I consider as the most precious gift of nature, for the instruction, the trusts, and government of society [Letter to John Adams, 1813].

JOHN F. KENNEDY

Democracy involves delays and debates and dissension. It requires men to think as well as believe, to look ahead as well as back, to give up narrow views or interests that retard their nation's progress. But given an opportunity to work, it completely contradicts and isolates the false appeals of the extremists who would destroy democracy [Speech in Rome, July 1, 1963].

ABRAHAM LINCOLN

Unanimity is impossible; the rule of a minority, as a permanent arrangement, is wholly inadmissable; so that, rejecting the majority principle, anarchy or despotism in some form is all that is left [First Inaugural Address, 1861].

JAMES MADISON

In a democracy the people meet and exercise the government in person; in a republic, they assemble and administer it by their representatives and agents. A democracy, consequently, will be confined to a small spot. A republic may be extended over a large region [*The Federalist*, no. 13, 1788].

JOHN STUART MILL

But the peculiar evil of silencing the expression of an opinion is, that it is robbing the human race; posterity as well as the existing generation; those who dissent from the opinion still more than those who hold it. If the opinion is right, they are deprived of the opportunity of exchanging error for truth; if wrong, they lose, what is almost as great a benefit, the clearer perception and livelier impression of truth, produced by its collision with error. . . . We can never be sure that the opinion we are endeavouring to stifle is a false opinion; and if we were sure, stifling it would be an evil still [*On Liberty*, 1859].

JAWAHARLAL NEHRU

Parliament and democracy are only considered desirable by the possessing classes so long as they maintain existing conditions. That is, of course, not real democracy; it is the exploitation of the democratic idea for undemocratic purposes. Real democracy has had no chance to exist so far, for there is an essential contradiction between the capitalist system and democracy. Democracy, if it means anything, means equality; not merely the equality of possessing a vote, but economic and social equality [*Glimpses of World History*, 1934].

THOMAS PAINE

Simple democracy was society governing itself without the aid of secondary means. By ingrafting representation upon democracy, we arrive at a system of government capable of embracing and confederating all the various interests and every extent of territory and population; and that also with advantages as much superior to hereditary government, as the republic of letters is to hereditary literature [*Rights of Man*, 1791].

POPE PIUS X

In performing its functions, Christian democracy is most strictly bound to depend upon ecclesiastical authority, and to render full submission and obedience to the bishops and those who represent them [*Apostolic Letter*, December 18, 1903].

HENRY DAVID THOREAU

The progress from an absolute to a limited monarchy, from a limited monarchy to a democracy, is a progress toward a true respect for the individual. Even the Chinese philosopher was wise enough to regard the individual as the basis of the empire. Is a democracy, such as we know it, the last improvement possible in government? Is it not possible to take a step further towards recognizing and organizing the rights of man? There will never be a really free and enlightened State until the State comes to recognize the individual as a higher and independent power, from which all its own power and authority are derived, and treats him accordingly. I please myself with imagining a State at last which can afford to be just to all men, and to treat the individual with respect [*Civil Disobedience*, 1849].

The Right to Revolution in Democracy

THOMAS JEFFERSON

What country before, ever existed a century and a half without a rebellion? And what country can preserve its liberties, if its rulers are not warned from time to time, that this people preserve the spirit of resistance? Let them take arms. The remedy is to set them right as to facts, pardon and pacify them. What signify a few lives lost in a century or two? The tree of liberty must be refreshed from time to time, with the blood of patriots and tyrants. It is its natural manure [Letter to William S. Smith, 1787].

ABRAHAM LINCOLN

This country, with its institutions, belongs to the people who inhabit it. Whenever they shall grow weary of the existing Government, they can exercise their *constitutional* right of amending it or their *revolutionary* right to dismember or overthrow it [First Inaugural Address, 1861].

JAMES MADISON

If there be a principle that ought not to be questioned within the United States, it is that every nation has a right to abolish an old government and establish a new one. This principle is not only recorded in every public

141

archive, written in every American heart, and sealed with the blood of a host of American martyrs, but is the only lawful tenure by which the United States hold their existence as a nation [Statement, c. 1788, quoted by Henry Steele Commager in *Freedom and Order*].

THE VIRGINIA BILL OF RIGHTS

Of all the various modes and forms of government, that is best which is capable of producing the greatest degree of happiness and safety, and is most effectually secured against the danger of maladministration; and that when any government shall be found inadequate, or contrary to those purposes, a majority of the community hath an indubitable, unalienable and indefensible right to reform, alter or abolish it, in such manner as shall be judged most conducive to the public weal [Virginia House of Delegates, 1776].

Marxists and Democracy

FRIEDRICH ENGELS

The first condition of liberty is that every official should be responsible in the ordinary courts and under the ordinary law, to every citizen for every act he performs in the exercise of his functions [Letter to August Bebel, 1875].

KARL MARX AND FRIEDRICH ENGELS

In short, the Communists everywhere support every revolutionary movement against the existing social and political order of things. In all these movements they bring to the front, as the leading question in each, the property question, no matter what its degree of development at the time. Finally, they labour everywhere for the union and agreement of the democratic parties of all countries [*The Communist Manifesto*, 1848].

VLADIMIR ILYICH LENIN

A democracy is a state which recognizes the subjection of the minority to the majority, that is, an organization for the systematic use of violence by one class against the other, by one part of the population against the other [*The State and Revolution*, 1917].

Take any parliamentary country, from America to Switzerland, from France to England, Norway and so forth—in these countries the actual work of the "State" is done behind the scenes, being carried on by the departments, the chancelleries and the General Staffs.

Parliament itself is given up to talk, for the sole purpose of fooling the "common people.". . .

The Commune substitutes for this venal and rotten parliamentary government of bourgeois society institutions in which freedom of opinion and discussion do not degenerate into deception, for the parliamentarians have to work themselves, to apply their own laws, to see for themselves what are their effects in real life, and themselves be directly responsible to their constituents. Representative institutions remain, but parliamentary government as a special system, as the division of labour between the legislature and the executive, as a privileged status for members of parliament, exists no more. We cannot imagine a democracy, even a proletarian democracy, without representative institutions, but we can and must bring it into being without the parliamentary system, unless our criticism of bourgeois society is but empty words [*The State and Revolution*, 1917].

How can one be a democrat and at the same time oppose the dictatorship of the proletariat? [*Pravda*, May 12, 1917]

The "broad democratic principle," as everyone will probably agree, presupposes two conditions—first, full publicity, and secondly, election to all offices. Democracy without full publicity—a publicity reaching beyond the organization's own members—is inconceivable. We call the German Socialist Party a democratic organization because all its activities—even its party congresses —are conducted in public. But an organization that is hidden from everyone but its members by a veil of secrecy cannot be called democratic. . . .

The second criterion of democracy, the principle of election, . . . is taken for granted in politically free countries. "The members of the Party are those who accept the principles of the Party programme and render the Party all possible support," reads Clause I of the Rules of the German Social Democratic Party.

Since everyone can view the political arena as an audience views a theatre stage, everyone knows, from the press and through public meetings, whether a particular person accepts the party or not, whether he supports or opposes it. Everyone knows how a certain political figure set out in life, what phases he passed through, how he behaved in a crisis and what qualities he possesses; consequently, *all* party members, knowing all the facts, can elect him to a particular party office or not. The general control (in the literal sense of the term) exercised over all that a party man does in his political career brings into existence an automatic mechanism which produces what in biology is called "the survival of the fittest." "Natural selection" by full publicity, election and general control ensures that, in the last analysis, every political figure will be "in his proper place," do the work for which he is best fitted by his powers and abilities, take the consequences of his mistakes himself, and prove before all the world his ability to recognize mistakes and avoid them.

Just try to fit this picture into the frame of our autocracy! [*What is to Be Done?* 1902].

ROSA LUXEMBURG

It is clear that socialism by its very nature cannot be decreed. . . . Without general elections, without unrestricted freedom of press and assembly, without a free struggle of opinion, life dies out in every public institution, becomes a mere semblance of life, in which only the bureaucracy remains as the active element. Public life gradually falls asleep, a few dozen party leaders of inexhaustible energy and boundless experience direct and rule [*The Russian Revolution*, 1918].

Weaknesses, Threats, and Warnings

JOHN ADAMS

Democracy never lasts long. It soon wastes, exhausts and murders itself. There never was a democracy yet that did not commit suicide [Attributed statement, c. 1785].

There is nothing I dread so much as the division of the Republic into two great parties each arranged under its leader.... This in my humble apprehension is to be dreaded as the greatest political evil under our Constitution [Letter to Jonathan Jackson, 1780].

KONRAD ADENAUER

God, in creating man, has hit upon a very poor compromise. If He had made man more intelligent, he would have known how to behave. If He had made man less intelligent, he would have been easier to govern [Attributed statement, c. 1960].

WILLY BRANDT

Western Europe has only twenty or thirty years of democracy left in it. After that it will slide, engineless and rudderless, under the surrounding sea of dictatorship and whether the dictation comes from a politburo or a junta will not make that much difference [Attributed statement, c. 1973].

JAMES BUCHANAN

Next in importance to the maintenance of the Constitution and the Union is the duty of preserving the Government free from the taint or even the suspicion of corruption. Public virtue is the vital spirit of republics, and history proves that when this has decayed and the love of money has usurped its place, although the forms of the free government may remain for a season, the substance has departed forever [Inaugural Address, 1857].

GEORGE GORDON, LORD BYRON

An aristocracy of blackguards. . . . The devil was the first democrat [*Diary*, May 1821].

ALEXIS DE TOCQUEVILLE

The manufacturing aristocracy which is growing up under our eyes is one of the harshest that ever existed in the world. . . . The friends of democracy should keep their eyes anxiously fixed in this direction; for if ever a permanent inequality of conditions and aristocracy again penetrates into the world, it may be predicted that this is the gate which they will enter [*Democracy in America*, 1835].

DWIGHT D. EISENHOWER

In the councils of government, we must guard against the acquisition of unwarranted influence, whether sought or unsought, by the military-industrial complex. The potential for the disastrous rise of misplaced power exists and will persist [Farewell Address, 1961].

MOHANDAS (MAHATMA) GANDHI

Our tyranny, if we impose our will on others, will be infinitely worse than that of the handful of Englishmen who form the bureaucracy. Theirs is a terrorism imposed by a minority struggling to exist in the midst of opposition. Ours will be a terrorism imposed by a majority and therefore worse and really more godless than the first. We must therefore eliminate compulsion in any shape from our struggle. If we are only a handful holding freely the doctrine of non-co-operation, we may have to die in the attempt to convert others to our view, but we shall have truly defended and represented our cause. If however, we enlist under our banner men by force, we shall be denying our cause and God, and if we seem to succeed for the moment, we shall have succeeded in establishing a worse terror [*Young India*, October 27, 1921].

ELBRIDGE GERRY

The evils we experience flow from the excess of democracy. The people do not want virtue, but are the dupes of pretended patriots [Speech in the Constitutional Convention, 1787].

ALEXANDER HAMILTON

Give all power to the few and they will oppress the many; give all power to the many and they will oppress the few [Speech in the Constitutional Convention, 1787].

It has been observed that a pure democracy, if it were practicable, would be the most perfect government. Experience has proved that no position is more false than this. The ancient democracies, in which the people themselves deliberated, never possessed one feature of good government. Their very character was tyranny; their figure deformity [Speech in the United States Senate, June 21, 1788].

KLEMENS METTERNICH

Ten million ignorances do not constitute one knowledge [Attributed statement, c. 1848].

DANIEL PATRICK MOYNIHAN

Democracies are becoming a recessive form of government, like monarchies used to be—something the world is moving from, rather than to. We've taken enough punishment lately to wake ourselves up and realize we may be in trouble [Speech in New York, 1975].

BENITO MUSSOLINI

Democracy is a kingless regime infested by many kings who are sometimes more exclusive, tyrannical, and destructive than one, if he be a tyrant [Speech in Rome, c. 1926].

Democracy is talking itself to death. The people do not know what is best for them. There is too much foolishness; too much lost motion [Interview in the *New York Times*, 1928].

JAWAHARLAL NEHRU

Men like Jawaharlal, with all their capacity for great and good work, are unsafe in a democracy. He calls himself a democrat and a socialist and no doubt he does so in all earnestness, but every psychologist knows that the mind is ultimately a slave to the heart and that logic can always be made to fit in with the desires and irrepressive urges of man. A little twist and Jawaharlal might turn a dictator, sweeping aside the paraphernalia of a slow moving democracy [Anonymous article by and on himself, *Morning Review*, 1937].

JEAN-JACQUES ROUSSEAU

If there were a nation of gods they would be governed democratically, but so perfect a government is not suitable to man [*Du contrat social*, III, 1762].

BERTRAND RUSSELL

Envy is the basis of Democracy [*The Conquest of Happiness*, 1930].

GEORGE BERNARD SHAW

Democracy substitutes election by the incompetent many for appointment by the corrupt few [*Maxims for Revolutionaries*, 1903].

FRANÇOIS-MARIE VOLTAIRE

Democracy seems suitable only to a very little country [*Philosophical Dictionary*, 1764].

GEORGE WASHINGTON

There is an opinion that parties in free countries are useful checks upon the administration of the government, and serve to keep alive the spirit of liberty. This within certain limits is probably true; and in governments of a monarchical cast patriotism may look with indulgence, if not with favor, upon the spirit of party. But in those of the popular character, in governments purely elective, it is a spirit not to be encouraged [Farewell Address, 1796].

They [all the parts of our country, combined] will avoid the necessity of those overgrown military establishments which, under any form of government, are inauspicious to liberty, and which are to be regarded as particularly hostile to republican liberty [Farewell Address, 1796].